SPC LIBRARY
Exploring the concept of mind
BF 149 E86 1986

3 6854 00001050 2

SO-ARM-199

Ra I   15.95

WITHDRAWN

EXPLORING THE
CONCEPT OF MIND

BF
149
E86
1986

Exploring the Concept of Mind

Edited by Richard M. Caplan

University of Iowa Press  Iowa City

University of Iowa Press, Iowa City 52242
Copyright © 1986 by the University of Iowa
"How Old Is Consciousness?" copyright © 1986 by Julian Jaynes
All rights reserved
Printed in the United States of America
First edition, 1986

Book design by Patrick Hathcock
Jacket design by Richard Hendel
Typesetting by G & S Typesetters, Inc., Austin, Texas
Printing and binding by Edwards Brothers, Inc., Ann Arbor, Michigan

No part of this book may be reproduced or utilized in any form or by any means,
electronic or mechanical, including photocopying and recording, without permission
in writing from the publisher.

The symposium Exploring the Concept of Mind was supported by the University of
Iowa, the Stanley–University of Iowa Foundation Support Organization, the Program
in Medical Humanities at the University of Iowa College of Medicine, the Iowa Humanities Board, and the National Endowment for the Humanities. The opinions, findings, and conclusions in this book do not necessarily represent the views of the Iowa
Humanities Board or the National Endowment for the Humanities.

Library of Congress Cataloging-in-Publication Data
  Main entry under title:
  Exploring the concept of mind.
  1. Psychology—Addresses, essays, lectures.
I. Caplan, Richard M., 1929–   .
BF149.E86 1986 150 85-23228
ISBN 0-87745-144-3

Dedicated to the memory of my parents

Contents

Acknowledgments

The existence of this book owes a debt to far more than those distinguished persons whose words and thoughts are printed here following mine. Those others merit this additional message of appreciation.

Foremost is my colleague Sandra Pellens-Meinhard, whose initial ideas and energies prompted me and the rest of the enterprise. We were joined in planning the symposium by faculty members Laird Addis (Philosophy), Nancy Andreasen (Psychiatry), Gerald Bruns (English), Antonio Damasio (Neurology), James Hinrichs (Psychology), Richard Meinhard-Pellens (Education), Jay Semel (Administration), and Rafiq Waziri (Psychiatry).

At the symposium, faculty colleagues also delivered presentations which not only enriched the event greatly but strongly influenced me and my introductory chapter. This gratitude goes to Nancy Andreasen, James Hinrichs, Richard Meinhard-Pellens, Robert Baron (Computer Science), Michael Brody (Pharmacology), Timothy Eastman (Physics), Richard Fumerton (Philosophy), Richard Hurtig (Speech Pathology and Audiology), Roger Kathol (Psychiatry and Internal Medicine), James McCue (Religion), Marilyn Somville (Music), and Edward Wasserman (Psychology).

James O. Freedman, president of the University of Iowa, opened the symposium not only by introducing it but, because of his dedication to the humanities and to interdisciplinary effort, by stimulating the occurrence of an annual symposium in the humanities. I appreciate also the assistance of our several sources of financial support and the staffs of those agencies.

My office colleagues helped greatly with the activities of the symposium and with this book, all of which had to be crowded into our lives along with many other responsibilities. For that I especially thank Louis Crist, Jr., and my always cheerful and devoted secretary, Jean Dye.

My wife, Ellen, gave her usual unstinting help and counsel for which, as always, I am deeply thankful.

R. M. C.

Exploring the Concept of Mind: An Introduction

Richard M. Caplan

This chapter will respect its title by discussing, within the context of the University of Iowa Humanities Symposium of the same title, what *exploring* and *the concept of mind* mean. Finally, it will offer an introduction to the essays that follow. The section called "Exploring" will address the nature of the symposium and certain notions central to it, like "interdisciplinary," "language," and "metaphor," but particularly the scope and relationships among sciences and humanities. "The Concept of Mind" will elaborate on historical events, the mind-body problem, notions of cognition, creativity, and biology, and how our understanding can be enriched and advanced to a new level of abstraction. And finally this chapter will complete the implication of its title by introducing the specific themes to be discussed by the authors who follow. Their various concepts of mind, influenced by their personal experiences and disciplines, compose a band or array of color such as a prism produces when it refracts a beam of white light. The reader may be able to fuse those colors and experience at least briefly a sense of the pure light called truth or insight; but if not, just experiencing the separate colors for their own richness will bring its own delight.

Exploring

If the ancient but debatable claim is correct, that rationality defines us as human, then the suitability of MIND as the topic of a humanities symposium becomes apparent. The topic—ancient, complicated, and endlessly fascinating—deserves frequent attention because of its ever-fresh importance and because of the present swirling growth in the humanistic interpretations and scientific data that bear upon it.

So central to university life are the conceptions and manifestations of mind, that we often characterize a university as a place where scholars teach, investigate, and pursue the "life of the mind." That special life concerns such questions as the history and nature of knowing, the status of consciousness, the mechanisms of thinking and feeling, the structure and activity of the brain, the role of heredity and environment; further, it debates, bubbles, even froths, with such key terms as *language, cognition, dualism, behavior, neuroscience, speech, pain, metaphor, soul, mental illness, natural and artificial intelligence, memory, spirit, creativity,* and *reality.*

The symposium, through its structure, sought to explore the concept of mind through a series of illuminations projected by an unusual diversity of experts. While attempting to magnify certain new details of thinking and research, the essays in this book provide a more broadly rounded sense of the major themes and contours and make it easier to understand how some persons might argue that mind is everything, whereas others may argue as passionately and eloquently that there's no such thing as mind. I believe a multidisciplinary effort—even better, an interdisciplinary one—will bear fruit after its varied perspectives excite and cross-pollinate one another to produce vigorous hybrids.

The symposium was not only interdisciplinary but so *highly* so that some friends and counsellors warned me it made no sense to attempt such breadth; that instead, the symposium should convene a carefully chosen group of scholars who all work at the cutting edge of one small zone under this broad canopy called mind. Let such scholars address one another, said my counsellors, and then real progress in our knowledge and intellectual agenda might occur. I understand that point of view, but held more strongly for the benefits that would come from sharing across disciplines. That view highlights one of the deepest parts of whatever gulf separates humanities and sciences: the widespread conceit—perhaps especially dear to scientists—that humanities discussions don't *settle things* and that scientific inquiry *does.* Uttered from either camp, such notions are naive, simplistic. We all, speakers or readers, engage vigorously in the efforts we call mental, and those efforts will doubtless continue for as long as our species may endure.

This collection indeed tests how far the concept of *humanities* may be stretched. Those who conceive of the humanities as a traditional cluster of particular disciplines—namely, philosophy, history, literature, and languages—will feel that the definition should exclude other disciplines (such as psychology, anthropology, political science, music, education, religious studies) that also happen often to abide in a College of Liberal Arts, and most certainly should exclude the "hard" sciences of chemistry and physics and the "slightly softer" sciences of biology and medicine. On the other hand, some are guided by a broader and older definition of *humanities* that includes study of, and delight in, the human species and the richness of its abundant activities, thoughts, and feelings about itself and the world it inhabits. Obviously, the second definition guided the development of this symposium. Part of the exploring that occurred therefore concerned not only the concept of mind, but the process of interdisciplinary communication.

C. P. Snow's *The Two Cultures* (Snow 1959) gained enormous popularity through describing an essentially bimodal world of scholars. Many thinkers agreed that Snow drew attention usefully to an undesirable circumstance, and thus for the past twenty-five years there has been much effort to bridge the gap. More recently, some have reacted against Snow's view by saying, in effect, that the dichotomy he posited between science and humanities (or science *versus* humanities) never existed, and that his description polarized the two camps, thus exacerbating the very circumstance he deplored. There are also those who have felt that his description is too limited—that *all* disciplines roost on their individual mountains and *none* can hold meaningful discourse with another. Whether it's better to conceptualize one gap or many, to conceive of gentle valleys or abrupt chasms, there do seem insufficient occasions when scholars attempt to inform and clarify for each other what their thinking and scholarly work is really about. Whichever position one takes in that "two-cultures" debate, the universe of scholars certainly contains much specialism, with vocabulary, methods, departments, journals, and meetings all tending to decrease communication among those scholars who, on the one side, think and follow their pondering through descriptive and quantitative experiments, and, on the other side, those who "only" think.

Howard Gardner predicts that "the biological sciences will eventually be able to offer a cogent account of . . . intellectual phenomena. . . . And yet, because psychologists and biologists inhabit different environments, the task of marshaling biology to explain human intelligence has barely begun" (Gardner 1983, p. 31). A clear purpose of this symposium, then, was to bring scholars from different disciplines into one room and allow them, if they would, to hear each other even briefly, to elaborate and yet clarify the richness of the concept of mind, but probably not arrive at a consensus. We hoped that such an encounter would foster yeasty thinking, stimulation, and communication that might even slightly advance the understanding needed for the progress we seek.

Some of the assemblage might have thought we were about to perform a ritual of the kind known from the Indian legend of the six blind men examining an elephant. That image is splendidly concrete and usually helpful, but it needs modifying here in some important respects. Easiest to note is that the number of examiners is greater than six. More importantly, our experts are not blind—they see very well indeed. Nevertheless, they may wear, or choose to wear, blinders that limit the acuity or breadth of their vision. Wallace Stevens has given splendid tongue-in-cheek expression to the need for expanding one's outlook:

> Rationalists, wearing square hats,
> Think, in square rooms,
> Looking at the floor,
> Looking at the ceiling.
> They confine themselves
> To right-angled triangles.
> If they tried rhomboids,
> Cones, waving lines, ellipses—
> As, for example, the ellipse of the half-moon—
> Rationalists would wear sombreros. (Stevens 1967)

In his welcoming remarks to the symposium, University President James O. Freedman recognized that

the participants . . . will be searching for a point of view at which a variety of disciplinary perspectives converge. Whether they be materialists or idealists, whether they see oppositions between mind and body or between mind and spirit, whether they compare mind with the central processing unit of a super-computer or with a pure white ring of light, the participants will be exploring a terrain so forbidding that even the discovery of a tentative path in a common direction will be a major achievement.

He also reminded his listeners of the unifying visions of Coleridge and Keats, and the final lines from Yeats's poem "Among School Children": "O body swayed to music, O brightening glance, / How can we know the dancer from the dance?"

The symposium did not promise to produce a crisp definition of mind, nor did it promise to answer such questions as "What is the mind?" or "Where is it located?" or "Are there minds other than one's own?" Those questions *seem* worthy, perhaps because their grammatical structure reminds us of other useful questions, but experience has taught that these particular questions are flawed. Listening to the discussions and thinking about these issues engenders a wisdom or satisfaction in its own way, similar to "explaining" a poem by saying, "A poem is." True, the person who wears the label *scientist* may feel malcontent at the "softness" and wish to seek an understanding that is "harder," measurable, operationally definable, more analytical. And there lies the genesis, or at least an example, of Snow's two cultures that don't know how to speak to each other. This symposium sought actively to make connections, to sense and create new meanings, to reveal opportunities that might increase mental, investigative, and educational collaboration, and ultimately to purge the narrowness that might lead a person from discipline A to say, "I could learn nothing from any person from discipline B."

Some writers are willing to be hopeful, along with me, if not frankly optimistic. For example, Edelson has asked: "Is it self-evident, however, that the sciences and the humanities have evolved so far apart from one another that they are incapable of breeding with each other to produce anything but the most monstrous and sterile of offspring? I suggest that successful mating with pleasing results is possible" (Edelson 1984).

While part of the solution to the "mind-body problem" may come from turning our backs on the dualistic implication of the question (to be discussed below), another part may come through our increasing understanding of language and metaphor and through the role of computers in information processing and artificial intelligence. Descartes clearly posed a dualism by saying, "The human body itself, when considered apart from the mind to which it is united, is nothing but a machine" (see Gilson 1937, p. 161). This has framed the debate for more than three centuries, but we seem to be turning away from the question as he phrased it. As the linguist Whorf has said, and the idea has reverberated in many of this century's analytic philosophers, "We dissect nature along the lines laid down by our native language" (Whorf

1956, p. 213). Dell (1980), in his description of how the Hopi language and language-determining behaviors raise conflicts for Western therapists, shows how the dualism customarily ascribed to Descartes can be shown to have its roots in Aristotelianism.

The reader will have noticed how metaphorical is the language I have here written and quoted. Such highly imagistic expression will continue through this introduction and the essays to follow, for there seems no other way to deal with these ideas. The search for meaning (which phrase may serve as a satisfactory synonym for *the human condition*) obliges us to advance understanding through analogy, simile, and metaphor. Rorty has asserted, "It is pictures rather than propositions, metaphors rather than statements, which determine most of our philosophical convictions." But he displays how metaphors (such as the notion that reality produces "representations" in the mind, which thus mirror nature) can be counterproductive, citing "the domination of the mind of the West by ocular metaphors" (Rorty 1979, pp. 12, 13).

The necessity, construction, behavior, and fruitfulness of metaphor in language and human development have been explored by many, including one of our essayists, Julian Jaynes, in his book devoted to the origin of consciousness (Jaynes 1976). The theory of metaphor will not be repeated here, but I insist that scientific readers, especially (who might tend to dismiss metaphor as merely an artifice employed by poets and consequently of little importance to their own work), must come to grant not only legitimacy but perhaps primacy as well to metaphor. Scientists, as distinguished from scientific technicians, engage in processes of imagination, synthesis, and criticism, blended with judgments about aesthetics, purpose, and value. The behavior of scientists, even if they do not bring self-scrutiny into consciousness, implies that they understand the role of language and symbolization in their enterprise—and thus that they employ metaphor much to their benefit. This is so whether they speak of "things of substance," like cell membranes, DNA, or quartz crystals, or "things of ideation," like memory, intention, or appreciation. In the chapters that follow, the reader will find metaphor in use both with and without consciousness, so to speak, and also as the topic of focused discussion (a sort of meta-metaphor).

One metaphor deserves special mention—the computer. Our essayists do not dwell on the computer or related work in artificial intelligence, but awareness of the device and its rapidly expanding role (in helping create a new paradigm, generating hypotheses and enriching our storehouse of metaphors) will naturally pervade this volume. Neuroscientists and cognitive scientists, for example, must consider whether computers work like the brain (or vice versa), while Doris Grumbach, for example, here eschews the mechanistic characteristics that imply for her an extreme reductionism she finds uncongenial to her sense of imagination and personhood.

Many persons applaud the work of chemists and physicists in elucidating the mysteries of nature and providing the technological advantages of modern, comfortable life, such as radar for airline safety, television for edification or entertainment, fertilizer for a more productive garden. Biologists, too, have become increasingly prominent in elucidating nature's mysteries. Advances in molecular biology that followed upon understanding the replication of the double-helixed DNA molecule have made possible astounding advances in medicine and agriculture, paralleling the intellectual and scientific explosions that came with the insights of relativity and quantum theory. And yet, those same applauding persons may resist contemporary efforts at mapping the brain or elucidating mental functions by thinking analogically or metaphorically about the computer. Such resistance may resemble that raised, for example, against pesticides or genetic engineering by people who realize that the technological residua of scientific knowledge are not panaceas but have carried at times a heavy price in their influence on people, families, nations, and all humanity.

Pessimists surely may be made, if not born. And thus—no surprise—some persons may respond to the computer by regarding it as too inhuman to serve as an explanation, tool, or metaphor for understanding the thinking, the feeling, the mind which we have persuaded ourselves represents the essence of our humanness. Small wonder that the issue is deemed momentous. Yet no one today would, in seriousness, judge the genus of phenomena termed *the computer* to be ephemeral. Short of an ultimate cataclysm, the world of the future will no more do without computers than it would do without mass communications, mechanized transportation, or electric power. Darwin's contentions about evolution and selective variation have yet to win their last battle among either sophisticates or novices, yet his contribution has surely changed forever the idea of man. Similarly, the computer—what we put into it creatively, and what we draw back from it as an analytic tool and metaphor—will surely help illuminate what the process of mind is, what it can do, and what it can become.

The Concept of Mind

Throughout the history of Western civilization since the pre-Socratic Greek philosophers, thinkers have pondered what it is to know and how knowledge may be gained and validated. Much of the thinking has tended to produce categories of opposite nature, for example, subject/object, good/evil, divine/mortal, and of course, mind/body or mind/brain, and sciences/humanities as discussed above. Many of these polarities, growing in part from our language forms, have been exceedingly useful. Some, however, seem to have produced consternation and generated many philosophical conundrums. This may be what has led one of our essayists, Hilary Putnam, to begin the preface to his work *Reason, Truth and History* by saying, "In the present work, the aim which I have in mind is to break the strangle hold which a number of dichotomies appear to have on the thinking of both philosophers and laymen" (Putnam 1981, p. i). The mind-body problem and its subsidiary questions depend on dualistic thinking.

The concept of mind is broad, yet deep. Its complexity derives partly from its flavor of self-reference. To ask "When we think, what is it that thinks?" or to imply the infinite regress, "If I think, and can think about thinking, then surely I can think about the thinking about thinking," is to invite despair. Yet the challenge, for many, is too great to be ignored. And the links with other questions about reality, relationships, substance, and purpose, for example, invite us to muster our most rational powers to work on the issues buried in the concept of mind. A neurophysiologist recently said of the brain, "If the brain were simple enough for us to understand, we would be so simple that we couldn't" (Weller 1983). To the extent that we choose to understand mind as different from brain, we can make a corresponding assertion about mind. It is indeed just that staggering complexity that makes possible the promise of an evolving sense of insight.

Yes, these statements of self-reference regarding the mind do have the frustrating feel of a "Catch-22" or the effect of an Escher drawing that loops eternally into itself. (One grows used to that feeling with this topic, maybe even comes to find it titillating.)

An elegant telling of the history of the answers that have been offered through the ages regarding the location of the mind can be read in Critchley (1979). An eminent British neurologist, he skillfully combines many historical assertions that now seem humorous with Shakespeare's inquiry ("Tell me where is fancy bred; or in the heart, or in the head?") or Voltaire's scathing criticism ("Four thousand volumes of metaphysics will not teach us what the soul is. . . . I am persuaded that if a peacock could speak, he would boast of his soul, and would affirm that it inhabited his magnificent tail"). Critchley further speculates how the great physician of the seventeenth century, William

Harvey, "might have been astonished to learn of modern biophysical speculators who accept the electrical activity of neuronal circuits as adequate to account for all the manifestations of the human mind. But even the term 'mind' is outmoded in favor of 'neural dispositions.'" Many modern thinkers and scientists also rebel against the "bloodless dance of action potentials" and the "hurrying to and fro of molecules."

Aristotle believed the heart to be the anatomic locus of thoughts and sentiments, the brain simply a structure to cool the blood. As with other of his insights that we no longer accept, however, his views held sway incredibly long. (We do believe him yet in some particulars. I've heard no one suggest he was in error in stating that all men are mortal, or that Socrates was a man, or in concluding that Socrates was mortal.) When the brain came to be acknowledged as the site of those events and processes we now term mind, the great puzzle of *mechanism* arose, continuing since as a source of speculation and scientific work.

Foucault observed the entry into the skull thus, and we can feel his awe: "The fruit is then opened up. From under the meticulously parted shell, a soft, grayish mass appears, wrapped in viscous, veined skins: a delicate, dingy-looking pulp within which—freed at last and exposed at last to the light of day—shines the seat of knowledge" (Foucault 1973, p. xiii).

Physicians, too, if they pause to be reflective, have long expressed similar puzzlement and awe. And if they are good writers, they can convey vividly those reactions. In a fictionalized memoir, Arthur Conan Doyle's physician protagonist, Stark Munro, writes to a friend, "I ask myself, where is the man, the very, very inmost essence of the man?" After rhetorically subtracting from consideration great amounts of bodily material and arriving at the brain, he continues:

And now what is left? An arched whitish putty-like mass, some fifty odd ounces in weight. . . . This central mass of nervous matter may be pared down on all sides before we seem to get at the very seat of the soul . . . the spiritual part of the man. And what is left then? A little blob of matter, a hand-ful of nervous dough, a few ounces of tissue, but there—somewhere there—lurks that impalpable seed, to which the rest of our frame is just the pod. The old philosophers who put the soul in the pineal gland were not right, but after all they were uncommonly near the mark. (Doyle 1895, pp. 62, 63)

In "The Exact Location of the Soul," the contemporary American physician-author Richard Selzer describes a patient's brain this way: "Could this one-pound loaf of sourdough be the pelting brain? *This*, along whose busy circuitry run Reason and Madness in perpetual race—a race that most often ends in a tie? But the look deceives. What seems a fattish snail drowzing in its shell, in fact lives in quickness, where all is dart and stir and rapids of electricity" (Selzer 1974, p. 29).

In the preceding paragraphs I mentioned the words of Foucault, Doyle, and Selzer as producing puzzlement or awe. If readers could understand that such a thing was possible—that looking at ink marks ("puzzlement," "awe") on this printed page could truly evoke some conscious, internal sense—then they would be well along toward understanding that self, consciousness, awareness, thoughts, or even mind are constructs that arise from the activities and metabolism of neurons. Just as emotional reactions can be triggered by, but are different from, the printed symbols we read, or just as heat can be discussed, mutually understood, and bought and sold as a commodity without our needing to pause and remember that heat exists only by virtue of the motion of molecules, so minds, and all the other sticky words that adhere to the notion of mind, exist by virtue of the neurons and physical and chemical events that constitute their life. The next order of questions—for example, "What controls the behavior of the neurons?" or "How do they create the effects they do?"—will likely find answers through further scientific inquiry. The next level of questions beyond that—"How did life processes ultimately begin?" or "Have they any ultimate purpose?"—may never achieve a universally acceptable answer, but if they do, it will lie in the domain beyond science, that is, in metaphysics. A thinker crucial to the attempt to make metaphysics quantitative and move it toward what we now call modern science was Descartes.

Much of Western speculation and reasoning during the past three hundred years stems from Descartes, who wrote about feelings, thoughts, and emotions (passions) in his final work, *The Passions of the Soul*. His Latin word that we translate as "soul" was *anima*. The difference matters because we tend to add distinctively theological implications when we use the English word *soul*. Well aware of what it was to turn away from prior modes of thought, and consistent with the spirit of revolt that marked his epoch, he begins the work in this way:

There is nothing in which the defective nature of the sciences which we have received from the ancients appears more clearly than in what they have written on the passions . . . that which the ancients have taught regarding them is both so slight, and for the most part so far from credible, that I am unable to entertain any hope of approximating to the truth except by shunning the paths which they have followed.

As he begins his own exploration of the topic, he accentuates the crucial distinction we have so long accepted between mind and body:

There is no better means of arriving at a knowledge of our passions than to examine the difference which exists between soul and body in order to know to which of the two we must attribute each one of the functions which are within us. . . . All that we experience as being in us, and that to observation may exist in wholly inanimate bodies, must be attributed to our body alone; and, on the other hand, that all which is in us and which we cannot in any way conceive as possibly pertaining to a body, must be attributed to our soul. (Descartes 1649, p. 361)

How startling then to find him saying (Article V) that "a dead body loses its movement and heat not because the soul has left it, but to the contrary, the soul quits us on death only because this heat ceases, and the organs which serve to move the body disintegrate." A highly imaginative work, profound yet charming, that treats of the relationship among body, mind and brain, is Harding's "On Having No Head" (Harding 1972). The ideas there resonate well with the feelings and reactions generated by the Magritte image presented on the jacket of this book. Abolishing the head, as Magritte or Harding do, is a deliciously radical way to address a philosophical profundity.

In the science and philosophy of our twentieth century it is easier for us to understand mind as a function rather than an entity, and specifically as a function of body (brain). Maxine Greene declares herself always fascinated by John Dewey's notion that the mind should be treated as a verb and not as a noun. If we so understand the mind, then the mind-body dichotomy, or problem, largely disappears. We are left, though, with many difficult questions about the origin, purpose, and operations of this body and its ability to organize and regulate itself. Science, speculative philosophy, and all other disciplines have much yet to contribute to the continuing understanding of humans and the universe they inhabit.

Much of this discussion about dualism, Descartes, the relation of mind to the brain and its physics and chemistry, computers, and reality has been distilled cleverly by the contemporary cartoonist Berke Breathed, employing the anthropomorphic computer (see p. 12). It needs an electrical source and hardware, as well as a program to guide it; thus when its plug is pulled, the entire contraption is dead. And so it seems when people and their brains do what we call die.

This, then, is the central issue for those who wish not to posit some nonphysical essence, a noncorporeal substance or spirit that exists

BLOOM COUNTY   **by Berke Breathed**

Copyright © 1985 Washington Post Writers Group. Reprinted with permission.

apart from any corresponding pulpy, doughy, unromantic, palpable, pasty cheese that fills the cranium. On the other hand, to think that the splendors of perception, knowledge, fancy, ecstasy are *only* neurons, molecules of neurotransmitters, and blips of electrical discharge seems to belie the existence of anything else. The trap lies in the word *anything*, because it seems to oblige us to understand a mental event as a *substance* when what we need is to understand it as a *process*.

The switch from *thing* to *process* in understanding the relation between mind and body (mental events and brain) can be aided by knowing the enormously important and analogous change in world view that occurred early in this century when physicists were confronted with the theories and related data of quantum mechanics and relativity. Those hypotheses and their supporting experiments required physicists and philosophers to abandon many of their cherished beliefs derived both from Newtonian physics and from an atom that was conceived as an analogue to the Copernican solar system, with particulate electrons circling the atomic nucleus. Once electrons were understood, instead, as electrical charges—as events moving in fields of force, experiencing interchange with quanta of energy—then a new notion of matter, the fundamental "stuff" of the universe, was at hand.

The nature of that stuff had been the initial concern of Western philosophy: from Thales' pronouncement that all was water, to Empedocles' expansion of the list to include earth, air, and fire, and on to Heraclitus's paradoxical but more modern-sounding declaration that change itself was the only constant of the universe. Such effort to understand, whether by centuries of speculation and reason or by scientific experiment, has hardly brought us nearer to knowledge of a fundamental stuff. For example, a contemporary atomic physicist's review of the most fundamental descriptors of the physical universe enumerates thirty-four (including six leptons, fifteen quarks of diverse "flavors" and "colors," antiquarks, gluons, the photon, and distinctive forces), culminating in the disappointing speculation that even some of these entities may prove to be composites of still more basic entities (Quigg 1985). As physicists have continued their elucidation of intra-atomic structure (probably *behavior* or *processes* would better describe it) they have had increasingly to acknowledge the role of the perceptions and interpretations of human beings, whose interventions make possible, yet confound, their necessary measurements. Human mental processes and hypothesis-derived experimental intentions are thus found to be inevitable yet limiting to the understanding of the physical phenomena under study.

Ironically, while this more human or mind-centered awareness has been developing among physicists, biologists and psychologists have striven increasingly to understand the phenomena of their interest as objective events, almost Newtonian objects of reality that exist and behave apart from human interventions or attempts to measure and interpret. Bertrand Russell, writing in 1928, observes with wry pungency:

Physicists assure us there is no such thing as matter, and psychologists assure us that there is no such thing as mind. This is an unprecedented occurrence . . . [yet] what we can say, on the basis of physics itself, is that what we have hitherto called our body is really an elaborate scientific construction not corresponding to any physical reality. The modern would-be materialist thus finds himself in a curious position, for, while he may with a certain degree of success reduce the activities of the mind to those of the body, he cannot explain away the fact that the body itself is merely a convenient concept invented by the mind. We find ourselves thus going round and round in a circle: mind is an emanation of body, and body is an invention of mind.

He satisfies this conundrum by arguing that

the world consists of events, not of things that endure for a long time and have changing properties. Events can be collected into groups by their causal relations. If the causal relations are of one sort, the resulting group of events may be called a physical object, and if the causal relations are of another sort, the resulting group may be called a mind. Any event that occurs inside a man's head will belong to groups of both kinds; considered as belonging to a group of one kind, it is a constituent of his brain, and considered as belonging to a group of the other kind, it is a constituent of his mind. Thus both mind and matter are merely convenient ways of organizing events. There can be no reason for supposing that either a piece of mind or a piece of matter is immortal. (Russell 1935, pp. 170, 171)

What does this suggest regarding the nature of mind? (Note the important difference between *mind* and *the mind*; just dropping the definite article may advance our understanding greatly.) Can we accept mind to be the subjective, internal sense of the biochemical and biophysical processes of the brain? An old metaphor conceives of thoughts as the secretions of the brain, just as insulin is a secretion of the pancreas. This may be helpful, but it suggests that a thought is a substance, because insulin is, and that we might thereby collect a vial of pure thought.

Popper has proposed that mind is a *process* that generates *products* (Popper and Eccles 1977). In this sense the wheel, the theorems of Euclid, the Mona Lisa, or even a box of toilet tissue, Popper argues, are products. Since people believe the wheel was invented, the Mona Lisa was painted, and so on, we tend, when we speak of products, to beguile ourselves, by the very nature of language that thought is an inventor, a maker, a substance, a homunculus, even a god. We might, along with Popper and others, more accurately understand these products as stemming from mental processes.

Some important debates in the history of science may help illuminate the process question through their own analogical power. Phlogiston, a substance presumed to reside within any combustible material, was believed to be liberated during combustion and to leave behind a product much different and much lighter than the original. Since the early nineteenth century, after oxygen was discovered, atomic theory elaborated, and the total products of combustion more carefully analyzed and weighed, scientists have no longer believed in the existence of phlogiston, although, as Kuhn has rightly observed, no one has ever *disproved* its existence (Kuhn 1970). We have simply stopped speaking of it, and instead, have asked other questions and pursued what he taught us to call a new paradigm.

A second example deals with the nature of heat, a concept more a part of daily experience than phlogiston. Arguments long waged over whether heat was a substance, akin to arguments about whether mind is a substance. We now easily accept the idea that although heat is something we experience directly, it can be understood best as an epiphenomenon related to the motion of molecules, itself discernible never by direct but only indirect mensurational experience. Such an understanding is certainly "scientific reductionism," yet in no way does that correspondence of heat to molecular motion interfere with, or nullify, our perceptual (or even poetical) experience of what commonplace discourse calls heat.

A still further example can be drawn from medical history: until about a century ago fever was considered to be a disease, whereas now we regard it as a sign (a representation, an epiphenomenon) of an enormous variety of bodily disorders. Rather than a disease, fever is now readily understood as a symptom that bears a correspondence to pathophysiologic events.

But if we turn back to the mind, how may we explain the "awareness" of brain processes. Yes, the beating of the heart (and contraction of all other muscles, too) is associated with electrical discharges, as is the functioning of the brain. Yet we customarily have no *awareness* (consciousness) of the beat, unless it becomes extremely rapid, forceful, or irregular. Even then, however, it is not the heart which experiences the awareness of its own disordered beating. Rather, the brain, in its monitoring function, "senses" what is happening and "informs us" (we become aware). We never have a consciousness of heart or brain activity as being electrical discharges, per se, nor do we ever have direct awareness that cells of our pancreas are making and releasing insulin, that cells in our skin are growing hair, or that primordial cells in our bone marrow are busily producing offspring cells to circulate in the blood. Though we lack consciousness of these activities, we can measure the insulin or the growth of hair or the production of blood cells and through such indirect means know the behavior of these other parts of the body.

When pancreatic cells respond to increased amounts of glucose in the blood by manufacturing more insulin, should we conclude that the cells are *aware* of the increased sugar and *decide* to generate and release more insulin—or are those behavioral responses preprogrammed, totally and truly unconscious? When white blood cells swarm to an area of invading bacteria and engulf and digest the "enemy," is all that "military" action truly unconscious or do those cells somehow "know" what they are doing, and maybe even why? (Readers interested in a fuller exposition of how we employ military metaphors will enjoy Sontag's elaboration in *Illness as Metaphor* [Sontag 1977, pp. 64ff.].) We presently have no evidence to suggest such consciousness, but this is not to deny that at some future day—now existing only in flights of science fiction fantasy—we may develop instruments of appropriate discerning ability ("cleverness") to measure what might then deserve to be called consciousness.

Our brain now has the ability to monitor its own processes, at least a few of them, and we speak of that ability as self-consciousness (Popper and Eccles 1977, p. 35). The entry of the word *self* into the discussion causes the Nobel Prize–winning neuroscientist Eccles to proclaim himself a dualist, or at least an "interactionist." *But can one not have unity, rather than duality, simply by granting self-awareness as a characteristic quality of various brain processes?* More than one hundred years ago Ferrier wrote, "The physiological and the psychological are but different aspects of the same anatomical substrate" (Ferrier 1878, p. 3). Freud, the great archeologist of the mind, expressed a similar notion this way: "We must recollect that all our provisional ideas in psychology will presumably one day be based on an organic substructure" (Konner 1982, p. xv). Is it necessary, however, to conclude that all domains of sentient life, including moral and religious beliefs, are based in physiological events or are preprogrammed through Darwinian processes? One may prefer to believe, along with Eccles, that a sort of dualism can exist that offers hope of a something—a soul, a spirit—that transcends the brain and the bodily processes we now apprehend. To believe so seems to involve accepting the existence of something supernatural, some external or cosmic consciousness, some divinity, perhaps, or at least some controlling mechanism (not necessarily inimical to a scientist); but a sticking point comes if such a mechanism would be unobliged to obey what modern scientists understand to be the laws of nature. Granted, scientists readily admit that some of these laws remain to be discovered, but the belief persists intact that when they are found, they will operate without exception, capriciousness, or irrationality.

That word *belief*, in reference to science, is often forgotten by scientists themselves, just as it is seldom understood by laymen. Scientists and others must come to acknowledge that the enterprise of science is a system of values and beliefs as well as methods and findings, a means of pursuing knowledge that rests, ultimately, upon subjectivity and unverifiable assumptions. Science, by its methods, cannot *prove* its own correctness as a method of obtaining or verifying knowledge. It can assert, and knows how to provide probability statements about the likelihood of its assertions being correct. It is inherently ready, and eager, to yield to new assertions when new data arrive. Gardner has put it this way: "In addition to whatever superstitious, mystical or religious beliefs many of us hold onto unswervingly, an overall belief in science can be viewed as a kind of a myth, one that scientists are as loath to relinquish as our nonscientific brethren are reluctant to abandon their own mythic-poetic systems" (Gardner 1983, p. 31). He then draws even more sharply the relativity of the scientific method that serves as our base of knowledge of the physical universe. All this does not mean that we cannot function. After all, we can build a building and reasonably expect it to remain standing for all the time that will ever concern us, without insisting that the earth is flat, fixed, and absolutely unmoving. That battle was fought for us and won by Copernicus and Galileo. We will all be advanced if we understand science and its methods as a means of knowing some kinds of information regarding some of the questions and concerns of people and the world they inhabit. Physician/biologist/author Lewis Thomas alludes to this functional congruence of science and nonscience when he writes of "my contention that poetry and science are the same enterprise" (Thomas 1980).

The ultimate solution to the mind-body problem, the dualism of Descartes, or the materialistic reductionism of some contemporary thinkers may not be a productive problem or one that is solvable through traditional language and insights. We may finally deal with it as we have other problems, such as phlogiston, by turning our backs on it as being a debate that has continued long enough to run dry, and we must ask questions and frame our sense of the universe in a new way. As we have conducted more and more the business of "routine science" (Kuhn's phrase) we have grown more technological, alienated, and desperate for a new paradigm, a new grand synthesis. Along with T. S. Eliot we can ask: "Where is the wisdom we have lost in knowledge? / Where is the knowledge we have lost in information?" (Eliot 1952, p. 96).

Throughout recorded history some thinkers and doers have been more progressive, more venturesome than others, and have felt impelled to persuade others to adopt a new position. Such efforts of persuasion have dotted the intellectual landscape always, inspiring and justifying belief in a new point of view. I referred earlier to Descartes' 1649 broadside against the views of the ancients. William Harvey, who published his epoch-making work on the circulation of the blood twenty-one years earlier (1628) and founded modern physiology in the process, knew his views would not be easily accepted. He therefore wrote an eloquent appeal for open-mindedness when he dedicated his treatise, dealing with the motion and function of the heart, to the members of the Royal College of Physicians, whom he addressed as philosophers—a title then more appropriate when natural science was a subdivision of philosophy:

For true philosophers, who are only eager for truth and knowledge, never regard themselves as already so thoroughly informed, but that they welcome further information from whomsoever and from whencesoever it may come; nor are they so narrow-minded as to imagine any of the arts or sciences transmitted to us by the ancients, in such a state of forwardness or completeness, that nothing is left for the ingenuity and industry of others; very many, on the contrary, maintain that all we know is still infinitely less than all that still remains unknown; neither do they think it unworthy of them to change their opinion if truth and undoubted demonstration require them so to do; nor do they esteem it discreditable to desert error, though sanctioned by the highest antiquity; for they know full well that to err, to be deceived, is human; that many things are discovered by accident, and that many may be learned indifferently from any quarter. (Harvey 1628, p. 7)

An Introduction

Philosopher Hilary Putnam, charged to place the concept of mind into a historico-philosophical context, chose to ask, "How old is the mind?" and then answered that what we seem to understand as "the mind" is remarkably new—perhaps only some three hundred years old. But such an answer cannot, of course, be like choosing foil c on a multiple choice examination. Mind, a complex web of notions, has grown upon a historical continuum that is still evolving, and so Putnam moves back to Aristotle, and then forward through the British empiricists that succeeded Descartes, to contemporary analytic thinkers, finally including his own contributions to the topic. He also reminds us that everybody's arch-dualist, Descartes, once surprisingly declared, in what Putnam considers a generally unremembered inconsistency, a unity of mind and body.

The problem of perceptions that indicate an external reality that is *out there*, and the philosophical problem of whether other minds exist, were especially important to the British empiricists and seemed to lead speculation and rationality into a cul-de-sac. Rescue indeed came, first through Kant, then from subsequent scientific studies, and in this century behaviorism and analytic philosophy tried to shift to a more fruitful paradigm. Putnam himself, an advocate of speaking across disciplines and attempting to break down such oppositions as fact/value, object/subject, moral sciences/natural sciences, seeks to help us nullify the polarization created by the question of whether mind is identical to brain traces (electrical and chemical) or "only correlated" with brain traces. An understanding of the mind-body problem (if one is willing even to acknowledge that a problem exists) must lie far beyond an understanding of perceptions and sensations merely as material events in the brain.

Newtonian physics, along with Descartes, is another of the "villains" of the mind-body problem because it encourages a dichotomy of mind and matter analogous to the erroneous dualism of waves and particles in physics. Modern physics now describes waves and particles as emergent aspects of common phenomena. These phenomena involve patterns of events and interactions that must be studied and interpreted by human minds. It thus makes no more sense to speak of pure, mind-free matter (body) than of pure, disembodied mind. This kind of analysis from modern atomic physics parallels the *process* notion, since questions of reference and perception depend not only on what occurs inside the head but on the transaction between human beings and their environment, a transaction Putnam characterizes not as a dualism or physicalism but something in between—a "commonsense empiricism." Newtonian physics, he adds, attempted a description of things as they are in themselves, apart from the mind. In contrast, quantum mechanics has brought us to understand an inextricable relationship of physical realities to observers (which must include, of course, their sensory data and internal perceptions). Physics doesn't claim to give a "god's-eye view of the universe," but only to describe what we can measure either directly or indirectly, and thus always must include the observer. Philosophy and science, Putnam contends, always change one another through their interaction.

In dealing with the age of consciousness, psychologist Julian Jaynes extends Putnam's discussion about the age of the mind. When in human evolution did individuals begin to be aware, or conscious, of mental events and develop a sense of themselves? Jaynes believes that such a development happened in the era around 1200 B.C., and he supports his hypothesis with an immense breadth of scholarly information (Jaynes 1976). Metaphor, which is of special importance throughout the history of psychology, looms large in his contentions, and so he spends considerable effort to elaborate its nature, showing its vital role in the development of language and all that grows from language.

Until relatively recently, Jaynes thinks, there was no interior mind-space or self-awareness, no self-image. There existed previously only an awareness of events, and during those epochs, in Jaynes's view, the brain's right hemisphere directed the activities of the left hemisphere by actually speaking to it via auditory hallucinations. Those voices of instruction and direction were attributed to gods or godlike beings. Jaynes admits that there can be no controlled experiment to prove this contention and grants that the circumstantial evidence of the sort he musters from linguistics, archeology, theology, anthropology, literature and myth, and other disciplines will have to be the major means of persuasion. Much debate hinges on the nature of the putative auditory hallucinations and how they may relate to the hallucinations that occur in mentally ill persons, something Jaynes contends is totally different from the guiding, generally friendly voice that at one time arose in the right hemisphere, and the loss of which gave rise to consciousness—"the analogue *I* narratizing in a mind-space." Hofstadter and Dennett agree that "there are at present no easy answers to the big questions, and it will take radical rethinking of the issues before people can be expected to reach a consensus about the meaning of the word 'I'" (Hofstadter and Dennett 1981, preface).

Popper (Popper and Eccles 1977, p. 30) is among those who believe that in humans consciousness developed before language, while Jaynes's argument requires the reverse sequence. Jaynes admits his theory to be controversial, but indeed it served the symposium splendidly by helping to identify the problems and terms, and move us toward a clearer notion of the relationship between mind and brain.

The relationship of brain, as a neurobiological structure, to mental events is more specifically addressed in the essay by Antonio Damasio. He brings the perspective, work, and cautions of a fully engaged clinician and investigator of neuroscience. Nobel laureate David Hubel has said: "Neurobiology is notable for the wide range of approaches and techniques that have been brought to bear on it, from physics and biochemistry to psychology and psychiatry. In no other branch of research is a broad approach so essential, and in recent years it has begun to be achieved" (Hubel 1984, p. 4). Damasio seems to agree, and takes the matter even farther, as in an earlier lecture at the University of Iowa: "The ultimate meaning of the brain/mind relationships we now glimpse will depend on the bridges that neuroscience establishes with the non-medical domains of the humanities— history, sociology, anthropology, philosophy, psychology, linguistics, and the world of the creative artist" (Damasio 1985).

Damasio is not among those who deny mental events or grudgingly admit they may be identical to physical events in the brain; he describes the physicality of the brain "as the generator of mental phenomena." He is also optimistic that the relations between brain and mind can be elucidated through scientific inquiry, even if we have far to go. This contrasts with the dour view of Popper and Eccles, who "think it improbable that the [exceedingly difficult] problem [of the link between brain structures and processes, on the one hand, and mental dispositions and events on the other] will ever be solved. . . . We think that no more can be expected than to make a little progress here or there" (Popper and Eccles 1977, p. vii). The making of a little progress here or there will more likely occur, Damasio thinks, not by studying gross brain structures like lobes, but by investigating smaller anatomical and functional units.

He also feels it possible and necessary to build a bridge between the neurosciences and cognitive sciences. Crick likewise recommends to cognitive scientists (especially behaviorists) the linkage to neuro-biology: "What the organism actually does we can learn only by ob-serving it. Psychology alone, however, is likely to be sterile. It must combine the study of behavior with parallel studies of the inside of the brain" (Crick 1984). Speaking in abundantly metaphorical language, Damasio furthers this interdisciplinary appeal, contending that "the problem is that of finding adequate, powerful metaphors."

While Darwin was greatly criticized for his alleged implication that humans were more closely related to lower forms (for example, apes) than to higher forms (for example, angels), and for pointing out the seeming randomness and purposelessness of natural selection, mod-ern neuroscientists and computer scientists who address the nature of intelligence are criticized for suggesting not that humans are too like animals but too like machines. Darwin's belief, that the difference be-tween man and higher animals is one of degree and not kind, may find modern echo in the relationship between animal/human brains and computers. Further study of animals' minds and the analytic, model-ling power of computers is likely to enhance our understanding of human brain structure and function, and the corresponding mental events.

According to the doctrine of epiphenomenalism, consciousness or mental processes accompany and are determined by brain processes but cannot influence them. Such a view is exceedingly difficult to es-pouse now that medical science of this century has mustered evidence linking experience, perceptions, and intentions to bodily changes. In-creasing knowledge of how the entire nervous system works and how it relates to the pituitary and other endocrine glands, to blood vessels, muscles, and essentially all organs, has helped elucidate many phe-nomena that had been studied under the heading "psychosomatic medicine." The word *psychosomatic* itself perpetuates the mind-body dualism. Maybe this is one reason it has become less fashionable, whereas the idea of unity of mind and body, (w)holistic medicine, currently captures the fancy of so many.

Pellegrino argues that "the findings of neuropathology, neurosurgery, and the physiology and pharmacology of the nervous system, are essential, for example, to any serious deliberation on the philosophy of mind or psyche" (Pellegrino 1977, p. 83). That spirit prompted inclusion within the symposium of a panel that explored first how events of the mind (probably) or brain (certainly) bring about changes in the muscular tone and pressure relationships in blood vessels throughout the body. The commonsense awareness of some connection was expressed by William Harvey in 1628: "Every affection of the mind that is attended with either pain or pleasure, hope or fear, is the cause of an agitation whose influence extends to the heart" (Harvey 1628). The implications for cardiovascular diseases are enormous. Correspondingly, we heard about many disturbances in organs other than the brain that produce perturbations of the brain, perturbations that manifest themselves clinically as overtly disordered thinking and behavior. Examples include hypothyroidism, many infections, drug or environmental toxicities, and pellagra.

Such circumstances drawn from modern clinical medicine provide a context for the essay by David Morris. He aids the attempt to fuse psyche and soma, and humanities and science, through an exegesis about pain—an occasion which demands, he proclaims, an encounter with meaning: "We must avoid the erroneous assumption that the experience of pain and the encounter with meaning are separate activities, one belonging to the body, the other to the mind." Both science and humanities, it can be argued, work through metaphoric modelling. What happens then to pain when it enters the zone of language?

Pain has engaged human analysis throughout recorded history. It can be approached as a challenge to philosophy, psychology, theology, anthropology, linguistics, literature and other arts, and certainly to medicine. Anesthesia and modern pharmacology seem to have produced certain types of miracles for pain, but a broader, more humanities-oriented effort will be needed for the understanding and reduction of suffering, as contrasted to pain.

As one may infer from the title of his most recent book, *The Mind's Best Work* (1981), David Perkins devotes himself to the study of creativity. Much of that effort has involved detailed and imaginative introspective processes. Crick, taking a harsh stance, has remarked:

Our capacity for deceiving ourselves about the operation of our brain is almost limitless, mainly because what we can report is only a minute fraction of what goes on in our head. This is why much of philosophy has been barren for more than 2,000 years and it is likely to remain so until philosophers learn to understand the language of information processing. This is not to say, however, that the study of our mental processes by introspection should be totally abandoned, as the behaviorists have tried to do. To do so would be to discard one of the most significant attributes of what we are trying to study. The fact remains that the evidence of introspection should never be accepted at face value. It should be explained in terms other than just its own. (Crick 1984, p. 15)

Perkins is trying valiantly to explain the abundant introspective data he has gathered.

Employing the metaphor of the mapmaker, Perkins essays to convey the shape of territories of intelligence and creativity, even though the borders are as indistinct as the relationships. A quest for creativity requires a discussion of theories of intelligence, which he clusters as power theories, tactical theories, and knowledge theories. His answer to the question about the location of intelligence—mind or brain—"yields an inevitable and uninteresting 'both,'" since he accepts a one-to-one correspondence between brain events and mind events. The computer metaphor then appears, as Perkins suggests that the distinction between mind and brain is something like the distinction between software and hardware, with the hardware of the brain being "the original equipment, perhaps improved by organic growth and development, while the software is the overlay of knowledge and know-how that gives the brain something to think about and with."

His analysis of creativity identifies six characteristics. Creativity depends on aesthetic as much as practical standards, attention to purposes as much as to results, mobility more than fluency, working at the edge more than at the center of one's competence, being objective as much as subjective, and intrinsic motivation more than extrinsic. Finally, Perkins relates intelligence to creativity by saying, "Creativity is intelligence with an accent." His summation is highly optimistic, for if creativity depends largely on tactical intelligence, as he believes, and thus relates more to mind than to the inherited and less malleable hardware of the brain, then it should be possible to train oneself and others to act creatively.

Reaction at the symposium to Perkins's analysis included distress with the computer metaphor. The worry emerged that the scientific approach takes things apart but may not find much reason to put them back together in interesting or significant ways. (In a practical sense that criticism may be useful by providing a social rationale for the artist.) To smell flowers, see trees, feel one's body move is to gather up feelings and experience. This resonates with the distinction Barzun draws between culture and scholarship, in which he charges that contemporary university values often regard scholarship to be an act of dissection, destructive to the sense of delight and awe or the wisdom to be had through a less analytical approach (Barzun 1984). Perkins's response to the charge of coldness (one might here say heartlessness, but surely not mindlessness) in scientific analysis was to recall Einstein's warning that "it is not the job of a chemical analysis of a cup of tea to taste like the tea."

Perhaps it may be said that psychologists and neuroscientists are more likely to be interested in the creative *processes*, while humanists may more likely attend to the creative *products*. Descartes thought the pineal gland, deep in the brain, was the locus where the physical entity he understood as body was integrated with the nonphysical entity he understood as mind (soul/*anima*); the seventeenth-century physician-anatomist Thomas Willis, memorialized for his study of blood vessels in the brain, thought the corpus callosum, the broad band of tissue that connects the cerebral hemispheres, was the seat of the imagination; and Doris Grumbach at this symposium captured her audience by describing the mind as "a compost heap, composed of everything one has heard, overheard, seen, imagined, dreamed, been told, read, remembered." Descartes and Willis *thought* they were being scientific; Grumbach *knew* she was being literary. It is easy now to declare Descartes and Willis wrong; it is far more difficult to say that of Grumbach, because one cannot declare a metaphor wrong, but only lacking freshness, richness, or helpfulness. Her extended metaphor of the compost heap proves abundantly useful.

Grumbach does not enter the mind-body debate. She accepts mental events and emotional responses and treats them in their own order of reality, not as "scientific, mathematical truth, verifiable and demonstrable, but fictional truth which is receivable and acceptable revelation about the human condition. . . . The analytic mind staggers before the mysteries and imponderables of the creative impulse." Her interest lies not in mechanisms of structure and function of the brain but in the lyric or ode arising from human experience and interchange. The moral significance of human behavior would evaporate if we were to believe that people were just so much biochemical machinery; one cannot hold machinery responsible for its behavior.

In the work generally credited as being the first book on occupational diseases, the Italian physician Ramazzini says:

A long train of diseases is likewise entailed upon the studies of poets, philologers, divines, and in time all writers and the other retainers to learning who are chiefly employed in the functions of the mind. Above all, it goes hardest with the poets, who, by reason of the fantastic ideas always present in their minds both night and day, are timorous, morose, and very lean, as their aspects testify. (Ramazzini 1700, pp. 391–392)

Medical science would no longer fully agree, yet a sense of mysterious relationship lingers. The poet Elinor Wylie has offered a sense of it in "O Virtuous Light."

> Sudden excess of light has wrought
> Confusion in the secret place
> Where the slow miracles of thought
> Take shape through patience into grace.

Because mental illness has long been thought associated with artistic creativity, Grumbach discusses the "creative madness," but not in clinical terms. Writers are not more mentally ill than others, but their frequent attributes (such as eccentricity, elation, depression, and unpredictability) she presents in a thoroughly humane and considerate fashion to help the rest of us not only understand, but feel, the anguish and exultation of literary creativity. It is Grumbach's compost heap that will produce whatever we shall come to know of one another. Although Euripides is said to have gone to a deep cave when he wanted to write a tragedy, mountaintop experiences seem seldom to happen inside coal mines, even though the light of insight or ecstasy may arise in the darkest, gloomiest of caverns.

Maxine Greene would have us be awake. She reminds us of Thoreau's aphorism "Moral reform is the effort to throw off sleep," and alerts us to the hazard of being "embedded in a kind of nondescript cotton wool" (Virginia Woolf) or being "sunk in the everydayness" (Walker Percy) of one's own life. She sees education, along with philosophy and the humanities in general, as major mechanisms to help minds become fully alert to the world which opens before us.

Greene uses Wordsworth, Joyce and Alice Walker to explore themes that would make us *mindful*, in the sense of "being aware" and also in the more literal sense of "having a mind that's full." Too often in the classroom, she feels, "the dominant focus on the cognitive aspects of mind, on the importance of logical and systematic thinking . . . tends to narrow the field of attention." Along with Howard Gardner (1983), who feels our society has placed excessive emphasis on two types of intelligence (linguistic and mathematico-logical) at the expense of the other five types he has described (musical, spatial, bodily-kinesthetic, interpersonal, and intrapersonal), Greene believes students could be challenged far more to become intellectual challengers themselves. She would seek to create "situations in classrooms [that] would mean overcoming subject/object separations, [that] would involve students directly in the quest to know."

Mind is different from knowledge. It is an activity that uses or changes knowledge. The notion that the individual is a passive recipient of information or experience—a remnant of the eighteenth-century notion of the blank slate (tabula rasa)—is giving way to the recognition that the organism does something with the input. This reflects the view in quantum physics that the observer is an absolutely necessary component of the occurrence. Such a notion corresponds also with the genetic (or developmental) epistemology of Jean Piaget, who attempted to blend biology (genetics, evolution) with psychology (cognition, behavior) and philosophy (ontology, epistemology). To Greene, "the true consummation of the growth of mind [requires the discovery of new meanings that] can be communicated in ordinary language within ordinary life. For some, the language may be gesture; for others it may be song; for still others, it may be quantification; for most, it will be verbal translation, extending the interpretations of the real." That is what this educational philosopher means by *waking up*.

Conclusion

Our authors recognize the difference between having the mind *do* what it can, and explaining how or why it *can* do those things. Some persons have a taste for mystery and prefer to remain in awe of what might seem the ineffable; others are more enthralled with making the ineffable "effable."

Our symposium might have explored the concept of clocks rather than mind. If it had, we might have heard complaints that *clock* is too broad and vague a notion and that speculative philosophy on the general question will prove useless. If we do seek to deal with the broad theme, then we will need a synthetic effort to meld the components and say what clocks are really all about in such a way that those who have not previously realized what clocks are all about could now do so. All of us use a clock to tell time, or perhaps we enjoy it as an object of craftsmanship and beauty; some, though, will be prompted additionally to speculate philosophically on the significance of time to man and society, or on the nature of beauty; still others will want to enter the clock, to dissect and analyze how it achieves what it does. The "man of affairs" will use the clock to avoid missing the train; the poet will rhapsodize on the nature of time or the beauty of the clock and its mounting; the engineer or scientist will explore its operating mechanism. Some, given to synthesis, will tell the time by the clock, but in addition will relate to it and value it in these other ways.

These chapters, if successful, will move many readers closer to becoming synthesizers. It must happen so, if we attend closely and think hard about thinking and what we mean by mind, for we could hardly escape the generation of new metaphors, the stretching of our experiences and sensitivities in new ways and new directions. These writings also mean to reassert the importance of humanities in our personal lives as well as in our scholarly or academic lives, through an unusual interdisciplinary criss-cross of gifted individuals who would exemplify and discuss our human complexities and impressive individual capabilities for growth in depth and breadth. Perhaps ontology has come to deal with becoming more than with being; perhaps also epistemology should be understood to be more about seeking knowledge than about knowing.

During opening remarks at the symposium, David Morris recalled Samuel Johnson's statement "A man is made by conversation." He then suggested an ethical sense in Johnson's statement: "A man is made, fabricated, created and brought into social existence by the act of conversing with others." The same theme, conversation, attracted the philosopher Richard Rorty as he closed his book *Philosophy and the Mirror of Nature*: "Philosophers' moral concern should be with continuing the conversation of the West" (Rorty 1979, p. 394). If he is right in thinking that "personhood . . . is a matter of decision rather than knowledge" (p. 38), and if these chapters make a strong case for a unity of mind and body, wherein mind is an activity, a process, generated by corresponding events in the brain, then the conversation of this book will be fruitful and will aid in continuing the conversation.

References

Barzun, J. 1984. "Scholarship versus Culture." *The Atlantic* 254:93–104.

Crick, F. 1984. "Thinking about the Brain." In *The Brain*, a *Scientific American* offprint, pp. 13–20.

Critchley, M. 1979. *The Divine Banquet of the Brain, and Other Essays*. New York: Raven Press.

Damasio, A. 1985. Second Presidential Lecture. Iowa City: University of Iowa.

Dell, P. 1980. "The Hopi Family Therapist and the Aristotelian Parents." *Journal of Marital and Family Therapy* 6:123–130.

Descartes, R. 1649. (1927, 1955). *The Passions of the Soul*. In *Descartes Selections*. Edited by R. Eaton. New York: Scribners.

Doyle, A. 1895. *The Stark Munro Letters*. London: Longmans, Green and Co.

Edelson, J. 1984. "Metaphor, Medicine, and Medical Education." *The Pharos* 47:16.

Eliot, T. S. 1952. "The Rock," Chorus 1, in *The Complete Poems and Plays* 1909–1950, p. 96. New York: Harcourt, Brace & World, Inc.

Ferrier, D. 1878. *The Goulstonian Lectures*. London: Royal College of Physicians.

Foucault, M. 1973. *The Birth of the Clinic, An Archeology of Medical Perception*. Translated by A. M. Sheridan Smith. New York: Pantheon Books.

Gardner, H. 1983. *Frames of Mind: The Theory of Multiple Intelligences*. New York: Basic Books.

Gilson, E. 1937. *The Unity of Philosophical Experience*. New York: Scribners.

Harding, D. 1972. "On Having No Head." Reprinted in *The Mind's I* (1981). Edited by D. Hofstadter and D. Dennett, p. 23. New York: Basic Books.

Harvey, W. 1628 (1931). *Exercitatio Anatomica De Motu Cordis et Sanguinis Animalibus (Anatomical Studies on the Motion of the Heart and Blood)*. Springfield, Ill.: Charles C. Thomas.

Hofstadter, D. and Dennett, D. 1981. *The Mind's I*. New York: Basic Books.

Hubel, D. 1984. "The Brain." In *The Brain*, a *Scientific American* offprint, pp. 3–11.

Jaynes, J. 1976. *The Origin of Consciousness in the Breakdown of the Bicameral Mind*. Boston: Houghton Mifflin Co.

Konner, M. 1982. *The Tangled Wing: Biological Constraints on the Human Spirit*. New York: Holt, Rinehart and Winston.

Kuhn, T. 1970. *The Structure of Scientific Revolutions*. 2nd ed. Chicago: University of Chicago Press.

Pellegrino, E. 1977. *Humanism and the Physician*. Knoxville: University of Tennessee Press.

Perkins, D. 1981. *The Mind's Best Work*. Cambridge, Mass.: Harvard University Press.

Popper, K. and Eccles, J. 1977. *The Self and Its Brain*. New York: Springer International.

Putnam, H. 1981. *Reason, Truth and History*. Cambridge: Cambridge University Press.

Quigg, C. 1985. "Elementary Particles and Forces." *Scientific American* 252:84–95.

Ramazzini, B. 1700 (1964). *Diseases of Workers*. Translated by W. Wright. New York: Hafner Publishing Co.

Rorty, R. 1979. *Philosophy and the Mirror of Nature*. Princeton: Princeton University Press.

Russell, B. 1935 (rpt. 1984). *In Praise of Idleness*. London: George Allen and Unwin.

Selzer, R. 1974. *Mortal Lessons: Notes on the Art of Surgery*. New York: Simon and Schuster.

Snow, C. 1959. *The Two Cultures*. Cambridge: Cambridge University Press.

Sontag, S. 1977. *Illness as Metaphor*. New York: Farrar, Straus and Giroux.

Stevens, W. 1967. "Six Significant Landscapes." In *The Collected Poems of Wallace Stevens*. New York: Alfred Knopf.

Thomas, L. 1980. Foreward to Holub, M. 1980. *Sagittal Section: Poems by Miroslav Holub*. Oberlin, Ohio: The FIELD Translation Series, Oberlin College.

Weller, M., ed. 1983. *The Scientific Basis of Psychiatry*. Philadelphia: W. B. Saunders Co.

Whorf, B. 1956. *Language, Thought, and Reality*. Edited by John Carroll. Cambridge, Mass.: The MIT Press.

How Old Is the Mind?

Hilary Putnam

In this century people talk as if the mind is almost a self-evident idea. It is as if the phenomena themselves required us to classify them as mental or physical in the way we do. Yet the present notion is not very old, or at least its hegemony is not very old. The words *mind* and *soul*, or their classical ancestors, the Latin *mens* and the Greek *psyche*, are of course old. The habit of identifying notions which are actually quite different leads us to think that therefore the present notion of the mind must be equally old, but nothing could be more false. This is worth knowing as a fact of intellectual history, of course, but my hope is that whatever our interest in the mind—whether as philosophers or as psychologists or as "cognitive scientists" or just as curious and puzzled human beings—we may find that this bit of intellectual history may also have the benefit of making usual ways of thinking about our "mental phenomena" seem less coercive.

Let us begin, as one so often does, with Aristotle. Aristotle's *De Anima* is often considered (rightly, I believe) the first work on psychology—indeed, it virtually gives the subject its name. But is Aristotle's subject, the psyche, to be identified with what we call the mind? (*Psyche* is often translated "soul," so we could also ask whether the psyche is to be identified with what we call—or have called—the soul.)

The answer, known to those of you who have read Aristotle, is no. Aristotle's *psyche* is the "form," or I would say the organization to function, of the whole organized living body. Its nature is that of a capacity. (A capacity is described as a "first actuality" in the standard translation of Aristotle's text; perhaps the thought is that the "primary realities," as one might also render "first actuality," are capacities to *do* things.) Among the activities of the psyche (activities listed by Aristotle) are those we would regard as mental (desire and thought), but also activities we would regard as physical (digestion and reproduction). These activities are the "second actualities." But our capacity for reproduction and our capacity for digestion are obviously not part of what we nowadays call mind. If the Aristotelian *psyche* corresponds to any contemporary notion it is to the extremely up-to-date notion of our "functional organization," as I have argued elsewhere (Putnam 1975a), but not to the present popular notion of the mind.

Aristotle has other notions, other distinctions; do any of these quite correspond to *our* mental/physical distinction? There is, for example, the famous notion of *nous* (reason). But the *nous* is much more restricted than the mind. The "passions," the natural desires for affection (at least for physical affection), for sustenance, for comfort, as well as the vindictive and aggressive feelings and the vanity and desire for admiration that are a part of our makeup, are none of them part of the *nous*. (In Plato's tripartite division of the soul, the passions were themselves a section and the *nous* was a different section.) The ordinary sensations of sight or hearing are also not part of the *nous*. (Sensation did not come to be considered part of the mind until very late. In fact, during the last two or three hundred years, especially in English-speaking countries, the mind has been virtually identified with sensation.) In Aristotle's system, visual sensations occur in the sense of sight itself, auditory sensations in the sense of hearing itself.

A point that is puzzling, or at least one that I find puzzling, is just how information from the senses gets integrated with general principles from the *nous*; such integration is required as much by Aristotle's account of theoretical reasoning as by his account of practical reasoning. But Aristotle does not describe the faculty that performs this task (*unless it is the "common sense"*?). He recognizes the need for an integrative agency, and locates it in the region of the heart. At any rate, one can generate questions about how *nous* is related to body, how *psyche* is related to body, and so on, within the Aristotelian system; and Aristotle says things about those questions (for example, he says "active *nous*" is separable from body but the psyche as a whole is not), but one cannot find the modern "mind-body problem."

Similar points can be made about the medieval conceptions. Aquinas had an elaborate psychology (Aquinas 1965), but it does not divide things up as we now do. The senses, in Aquinas's scheme, produce representations in the passive imagination, which Aquinas (using an Aristotelian term) calls *phantasmata* (not fantastic things, but perceptions). Like Aristotle, Aquinas considers these sensory images to be material (although not in a modern reductive sense—there is no talk of neurons or of computer circuitry in the brain, of course). To modern ears, this conception of the sensory images as something virtually on a level with body is, perhaps, the strangest feature of the classical way of thinking. Since British empiricism virtually identified the mind with images (or "ideas" as they were called in the seventeenth century), *we* have come to think of images as paradigmatically "mental," and—unless we are materialists—as immaterial. Yet for the classical thinkers it was reason—*nous*—that was unlike body, and sensation that was clearly on the side of matter and body. (In Aquinas's psychology the *phantasm* is explicitly described as "material," from which the intellect extracts an "intellectual species" or—to make one of those oversimple equations I warned against—a concept.)

One of the most difficult questions to answer about these models is the exact location of *memory*. It has come to seem such a central function of the mind to us that we tend to read it back into earlier writers. And until you actually look for it, you don't become aware of how very different thinking about memory was, just as thinking about sensation was very different. Earlier writers distinguished two kinds of memory. One kind is memory of things you can understand or see with your intellect once you've figured something out (for example, the Pythagorean theorem, or that the essence of being human is being rational). Once you've figured out one of these intellectual truths and come to grasp it, you can recall it, and it's in your *nous* itself. But if I have an ordinary memory of something that happened to me (say, that I ate eggs for breakfast) or of a fact about myself (my name is Hilary Putnam), where is this stored? Certainly not in the active *nous*. Neither Aristotle nor Aquinas is explicit about this, but I think that the following position might be ascribed to both of them: if I am not actively now recalling the episode or the fact, then the memory trace is not in my *nous* at all. Aquinas already knew that the brain and not the heart was the seat of the intellect; although it sounds strangely contemporary, the view that "brain traces" are memories which are not actively being re-called, might well have been perfectly acceptable to him.

Aquinas is not at all wedded to the view that you can think properly without a body. In fact, he explicitly denies that you can think properly without a body. He rejects the theology according to which the body is simply a kind of drag on the soul which corrupts it, drives it down, and makes it sinful. God, he believed, was a good workman. He made this body and this soul for each other; without one the other doesn't really work. If this interpretation is correct, then when I remember my name or what I had for breakfast, something in my brain activates my passive imagination and produces a *phantasm* (one from the inside instead of the outside); my *nous* acts on this *phantasm* and obtains conceptual information from it.

I said this view sounds contemporary, and up to a point it is. A mod-ern materialist who does not trouble himself to distinguish between mind and brain might feel that such a view was virtually just common sense. But notice that it is not quite the common-sense view. The con-temporary "common-sense" view is that it is obvious that memories are in the mind; what is still regarded as a difficult question is whether they are *identical* with brain traces or only *correlated* with brain traces. The view I have been attributing to Aquinas is that it is obvious that memories are in the body (the brain); when they are not actively being recalled, they are not "mental" at all. The *nous*/body distinction that Aquinas would have drawn is not at all the same as the modern mind/body distinction. Yet, when I think about it, it doesn't sound worse than the modern one! *Is it* obvious that there is something called the mind whose contents include all of my memories, whether I am actively recalling them or not, but whose functions do not include di-gestion or reproduction? Or are we in the grip of a picture, a picture whose origins are somewhat accidental and whose logic, once exam-ined, is not compelling?

The fact that the passions and the episodic memories (as opposed to memories of general principles, like the principles of geometry or logic) are not part of the *nous*, of the part of the mind which Aquinas considered to be immaterial, sheds light on a controversy concerning the doctrines of Maimonides as well as on some vexed interpretative questions concerning Descartes. Although in his doctrinal writings (his great commentary on the Talmud) Maimonides avows belief in immor-tality, in his work of pure theoretical philosophy, the *Guide to the Per-plexed*, he qualifies this notion in such a way that Strauss (Strauss

1963), in particular, has wondered whether Maimonides believed in *personal* immortality at all. Some of the things Maimonides writes lead Strauss to think that, in Maimonides' view, only reason, "active *nous*," is indestructible. If the active *nous* does not contain such things as memory of the episodes in my life, my knowledge of who I am, my desires (insofar as they do not stem from reason alone), and so on, then even if it be true that active *nous* is not destroyed when I die, this is not what anyone ordinarily thinks of as me, Hilary Putnam, surviving my bodily death. I don't wish to assert that Strauss's interpretation is right; but the very presence in medieval philosophy of this distinction between survival of the *nous* and survival of the *individual* illustrates how very different the immaterial part of the soul, as a medieval philosopher would have termed it, is from what we today call the mind.

The problem in Descartes to which I alluded is the problem of reconciling the statement that I am essentially a mind (a "thing that thinks"), which we find in the *Discourse* and the *Meditations*, with the statement in Descartes' letters that I am not my mind alone but rather an organic unity of my mind and my body. (That is a famous problem in the interpretation of Descartes, and most interpreters have suggested that Descartes was just inconsistent.) One possible way of reconciling the two statements would be to interpret the *I* that is my mind as simply the active thinking consciousness—there is no evidence at all that Descartes has an "unconscious mind"—and the *I* that is the organic unity as the whole self, including my memories, standing dispositions, and sensations. (For example, Paul Hoffman [1985] has argued that in Descartes' view sensations were material images in the body rather than "mental" phenomena in the Cartesian sense, and Hoffman takes this to support reading Descartes' view of the *self* as a true organic unity view. Note that if Hoffman is right, Descartes is, among other things, continuing the tradition that goes back to Aristotle, the tradition of thinking of sensations as "material.")

Humean Minds and Post-Kantian Minds

When I wrote my first paper on the mind-body problem, "Minds and Machines" (Putnam 1975a), I argued that a "logical analogue" of the problem arises for Turing machines, and that "all of the question of 'mind-body identity' can be mirrored in terms of the analogue." To do this, I imagined a machine which is capable of generating scientific theories, and which accepts theories that satisfy certain criteria ("assuming it is possible to mechanize inductive logic to some degree"). "In particular, if the machine has electronic 'sense organs' which enable it to scan itself while it is in operation, it may formulate theories concerning its own structure and subject them to test," I wrote. I imagined the machine discovering "I am in state A when and only when flip-flop 36 is on." Here "I am in state A" was supposed to be *observation (introspective) language for the machine*: that is, the command that the machine print out "I am in state A" when it is in state A is "hard-wired" into the machine, while "flip-flop 36" (machines had flip-flops and not circuit chips in those days) is supposed to be *theoretical language for the machine*. "Flip-flop 36" was described as a "theoretical term" which is "partially interpreted in terms of observables." I went on to assert:

> Now all of the usual considerations for and against mind-body identification can be paralleled by considerations for and against saying that state A is in fact *identical* with flip-flop 36 being on.
>
> Corresponding to Occamist arguments for "identity" in the one case are Occamist arguments for identity in the other. And the usual arguments for dualism in the mind-body case can be paralleled in the other: for the machine "state A" is something directly observable; on the other hand "flip-flops" are something it knows about only via highly sophisticated scientific inferences— How *could* two things so different *possibly* be the same? (Putnam 1975a, p. 363)

What interests me when I read the writing of my former self is how obvious it seemed to me that the mind-body problem concerned, in the first instance at least, *sensations*, and how the "usual arguments for dualism" were all arguments against identifying sensations with anything physical. Nor was I alone in this impression. A glance at the various anthologies on the mind-body problem reveals that it was just about universal in those years. Everybody "knew" the mind-body problem had to do with whether sensations were material or not. Obviously something had happened in philosophy—at least among English-speaking philosophers—between Descartes' time and ours to bring this about.

What had happened was the impact of British empiricism, and in particular the empiricism of Berkeley and Hume. The classical view was based, as I have said, on Aristotle, for whom there was something in common between my perception of the object and the object itself—exactly *what* is a difficult question of interpretation, and I don't think that Aristotle really worked it out. I think that when you try to read more into Aristotle's theory you are already creating your own theory rather than his. But at the least he says that the Logos (sometimes translated "Form") of the external thing enters into my mind in perception, minus, of course, the matter. I don't have a chair in my head if I look at a red chair, but I do somehow have the form, chair. Whether you have the form red is another question. Perceptions, according to the classical reading of *De Anima*, produce *phantasmata* in us (in our "passive imagination," in Aquinas's system), and these *phantasmata* were identified with what were later called "sense impressions" or even with mental "images." (Martha Nussbaum has argued [Nussbaum 1978] that this reading is actually a misreading, and that *phantasmata* are by no means always images; but this question is far too difficult to discuss here.) At any rate, the Aristotelian view holds that the "form" of the external thing is somehow connected both with the external thing whose form it is *and* with the *phantasm* produced in me by seeing or touching or hearing or smelling or tasting the thing. When I see a chair, the very "form" of the chair is in some way in me.

Descartes, however, argued that in the case of the so-called secondary qualities (texture, color, and so on), it is a mistake to confuse the sense in which a mental image can have one of those qualities with the sense in which a material object can do so. When I have a mental image or a sense impression of a red, smooth table, I may call the image smooth and I may call the table smooth; but there are two concepts (or "forms") of *smooth* involved here, not one. Similarly with *red*. In the case of the primary qualities—the "extension" of the material object, its size and figure—Descartes did, however, retain the classical view that these are present in the mind *and* in the object, that (in this respect) I have the very form of the object within my own mind (though not, of course, its matter). Now Berkeley pointed out that an image can no more be literally three inches long than it can be literally red in the way a physical object is red. In Berkeley's view—which became the almost universal view at once—a mental image or a sense impression has no ordinary property in common with matter: no physical length, no physical shape, no physical color, no physical texture, and so on. Of course, this is not how Berkeley himself would have put it. Berkeley would rather have said that the only red we know is the red we directly experience—which, in his view, is the red of the "idea," the sense impression or image; that the only smooth we know is the smooth we directly experience, the smooth of the "idea"; that the only extension we know is the extension we directly experience, the extension of the "idea"; and he notoriously went on to conclude that the whole notion of a realm of matter distinct from and responsible for our "ideas" is a philosophers' mistake.*

Although the philosophical world as a whole did not follow Berkeley into that immaterialism, it did follow Berkeley in concluding that (contrary to the classical tradition) sense impressions and images were totally immaterial. From Berkeley's time until very recently (if not still to the present day) it has been a minority view that, say, pains or visual impressions could possibly be identical with physical events or processes. The mind-body problem has become (among English-speaking philosophers) the problem of the relation of these apparently immaterial sensations (now thought of as the paradigm of the "mental") to the physical world.

In Germany, however—and German philosophy was the dominant philosophy in the whole non-English-speaking world until very recently—a different evolution took place. The dominant influence was Kant. Kant's views are extremely difficult, and I will touch on only one or two issues here. Kant addresses both what we today would call the problem of the nature of the mind—that is, problems of theoretical psychology—and problems of the nature of the self. (Most of his readers have tended to ignore the distinction between these two sorts of problems in Kant's writings.) There is, in Kant's system, a distinction between the self of pure subjectivity—the Berkeleyan "Spirit," which is always subject, always "I," and never object (the "transcendental

---

*Berkeley did not think the world consisted only of "ideas," however. The mind was not (as it became for Hume) just a collection of sense impressions, images of the imagination, memory images, conscious feelings, and so on. There were, for Berkeley, also the subjects of the "ideas." Subjectivity is irreducible in Berkeley's system. My "I," my "self," is a "spirit" (in Berkeley's terminology), and the world consists of "Spirits and their Ideas." The two categories of Spirit and Idea are correlative in this system: a Spirit is described by saying what its Ideas are, and Ideas, to be completely described, must be assigned to the proper Spirit. For Hume, however, a Spirit is nothing but a bundle of Ideas. (Whether this solves the problem of subjectivity or conceals it by hiding it behind the notion of a bundling relation has been argued by philosophers for centuries.) With Hume's step of identifying the mind with a "collection" (that ambiguous word!) of sensations and feelings and images, the transformation of the mind-body problem into what I knew it as in 1960, and into what my teachers and my teachers' teachers knew it as, was complete.

Incidentally, it is with Hume that memory gets classified as a part—or rather a faculty—of the mind: the faculty "by which we repeat our impressions" in such a way that

unity of apperception," in Kant's jargon)—and the empirical self, the self Hume found whenever he introspected. On the side of mind, there is a similar duality (although it is a mistake, I believe, to simply identify the two dualities in Kant). There are the mental processes we can study empirically, the laws of association and so forth; and there are mental processes, processes of "synthesis" as Kant calls them, whose nature Kant says we will "probably" never be able to discover. The fact that Kant uses the word "probably" is one of the reasons that I think it unwarranted simply to identify the faculty of synthesis with the transcendental self. (That we cannot discover the nature of the transcendental self is not just a matter of "probability" for Kant.)

Note that Kant does not say there are two "substances"—mind and body (as Descartes did). Kant says, instead, that there are "dualities in our experience" (a striking phrase!) that refuse to go away. And I think that Kant was, here as elsewhere, on to something of permanent significance.

If the discussion of the mind-body problem in this country has changed since 1960, it is largely because of the present centrality of computers and computer-suggested metaphors to our modelling of mental processes. And, oddly enough, the effect of this change has been to bring post-Kantian topics and concerns back into English-speaking analytic philosophy in a massive way. (I say back into, because they were concerns of English-speaking philosophy at the turn of the century—it was with the decline of pragmatism and idealism and the rise of logical positivism that English-speaking philosophy reverted to its traditional empiricist way of conceiving mind-body issues.) Today we see the term *intentionality* (borrowed from Brentano) everywhere. A popular book on the computer model, Margaret Boden's *Minds and Mechanism*, formulates its task in highly Kantian language as "providing a richer image of *machines* that suggests how it is that subjectivity, purpose and freedom can characterize parts of the material universe" (Boden 1981, p. 293). Evidently, the nature of the mind-body problem is once again undergoing a shift. The paradigmatic question is no longer "Is pain identical with stimulation of C-fibers?" but rather, "How can subjectivity, purpose, and freedom characterize

---

they retain "a considerable degree of their first vitality." Calling memory a faculty of course raises more questions than it answers; but Hume's chapter "Of the Ideas of the Memory and Imagination" occupies less than two pages of his two-volume Treatise (Hume 1978)!

parts of the material universe?" It is the Kantian mind rather than the Humean mind that we now want to understand.

The reason for this is simply that computer models lend themselves more naturally to speculating about these Kantian topics than they do to speculations about the nature of sense-data. But what are the Kantian topics?

Kant was concerned about the following puzzle: when I describe a thought as an empirical psychologist might (Kant was thinking of Humean psychology, but the point he was making has not become outdated), I describe it as a sequence of representations—images or words with certain causes and certain effects. I may find out a great deal of value by doing this. But there is one thing that I can never discover as long as I stick to this approach, namely, that I am dealing with something which has truth, value, freedom, and meaning, and not just causes and effects. That's the central Kantian question.

Here is an example to illustrate what Kant had in mind. If I think, "There are cows in Rumania," then, regarded as an event in the material universe, what I have produced is a list or sequence of words—noises, or subvocalizations, or images in my mind, or whatever. If I utter (or think) not the sentence "There are cows in Rumania," but the mere list of words *There, are, cows, in, Rumania*, I also produce a sequence of words—one with different causes and effects to be sure. But the difference between judging that there are cows in Rumania and producing a mere list of noises seems to be something over and above a mere difference in the causes and effects in the two cases. The judgement is, in Kant's terminology, an act of *synthesis*. And the problem about which, according to Kant, empirical psychology cannot tell us anything, is the problem of understanding synthesis.

I myself think that Kant was right, but his claim remains intensely controversial today. Ken Winkler has written of Berkeley that "like some other great philosophers" he "thought that philosophy would end with him; what made him great is not that he ended it, but that he made it even harder to avoid" (Berkeley 1982). One of the "other great philosophers" Winkler had in mind must have been Kant. The problem Kant raised here has indeed proved hard to avoid.

The Problem of Synthesis Today

The question that Kant bestowed to us as his legacy is a question as to just what the key question about the mind actually is. What should puzzle us more: that we have sensations or that we have "propositional attitudes"? The problem of synthesis has taken a number of forms in contemporary philosophy and "cognitive science." One form is a heated discussion over whether the study of the semantical properties of thought is a topic for psychology (in the widest sense) at all.

Two philosophers who have argued for many years that it is not are Wilfred Sellars and W. V. Quine. Sentences (whether I say them or write them or just think them in my mind) do, indeed, have semantical properties. The sentence "There are cows in Rumania" has the property of being true, for example, and it contains words which denote the set of cows, the extended individual we call Rumania, and the set [⟨x,y⟩| x *is spatially contained in* y]. The properties of truth and denotation, mentioned in the previous sentence, are paradigmatic examples of semantical characteristics. But the explication of these semantical characteristics is not a problem for psychology at all. Truth and denotation are not in any way derivative from the mind; they are rather derivative from language. According to Quine, "Immanent truth, a la Tarski, is the only truth I recognize" (Quine 1981, p. 180). (For a discussion of the influence of Tarski's work on Quine see my "A Comparison of Something with Something Else" [Putnam 1985a].) The way to define *truth* and *denotation* has been found by Alfred Tarski, in his famous "definition of truth." Sellars himself has shown us how to understand denotation and other semantical notions in linguistic terms. Chisholm, on the other hand, has argued that it is extremely implausible to think that certain signs are "language" apart from their relation to a mind.*

---

*The following letter by Chisholm (from a famous correspondence between Sellars and Chisholm (Chisholm and Sellars 1958) illustrates the opposing views:

August 24, 1956

DEAR SELLARS,
    The philosophic question which separates us is, in your terms, the question whether
    (1) "_____" means p
is to be analysed as
    (2) "_____" expresses [thought] t and t is about p.
    I would urge that the first is to be analysed in terms of the second, but you would argue the converse. But we are in agreement, I take it, that we need a semantical (or intentional) term which is not needed in physics.
    How are we to decide whether (1) is to be analysed in terms of (2), or conversely? If the question were merely one of constructing a language, the answer would depend merely upon which would give us the neatest language. But if we take the first course, analysing the meaning of noises and marks by reference to the thoughts that living things have, the "intentionalist" will say: "Living things have a funny property that ordinary

Philosophers and cognitive scientists who do think the nature of meaning is a problem for psychology have many different ideas as to how and why it is so, and correspondingly many different programs for tackling the problem. One school of thought, based at M.I.T., holds that there is an innate "language of thought" (Fodor, 1975). This innate language, "Mentalese," is thought of as having the structure of a classical (or "Fregean") symbolic logic—complete with quantifiers, and so on. The meaning (or "content") of a thought is somehow determined by the way that thought is coded in "Mentalese." This "content" determines the "conceptual role" of the item—how it is related to the outputs of various hypothetical "modules" or "mental organs" that Fodor postulates, but it does not determine its external world reference. Reference (and truth) are problems for philosophy rather than for psychology, on this view. (So Kant is partly right; part of what makes thought thought—that it refers to external things—cannot be seen as long as we stick to a "methodologically solipsist" perspective, and psychology, according to Fodor, must be methodologically solipsist.)

Certain other philosophers hold that the key problem *is* the problem of reference, and that this problem can, in principle, be solved by a kind of social psychology. The reference of a term (at least in basic

---

physical things don't have." If we take the second course, there could be a "linguisticist" who could say with equal justification, "Marks and noises have a funny kind of characteristic that living things and other physical things don't have."

Where does the funny characteristic belong? (Surely it doesn't make one whit of difference to urge that it doesn't stand for a "descriptive relation." Brentano said substantially the same thing, incidentally, about the ostensible relation of "thinking about," etc.) Should we say there is a funny characteristic (i.e., a characteristic which would not be labelled by any physicalistic adjective) which belongs to living things—or one which belongs to certain noises and marks?

When the question is put this way, I should think, the plausible answer is that it's the living things that are peculiar, not the noises and marks. I believe it was your colleague Hospers who proposed this useful figure: that whereas both thoughts and words have meaning, just as both the sun and the moon send light to us, the meaning of words is related to the meaning of thoughts as the light of the moon is related to the light of the sun. Extinguish the living things and the noises and marks wouldn't shine any more. But if you extinguish the noises and marks, people can still think about things (but not so well, of course). Surely it would be unfounded psychological dogma to say that infants, mutes, and animals cannot have beliefs and desires until they are able to use language.

In saying, "There is a characteristic . . ." in paragraph 2 above, I don't mean to say, of course, that there are abstract entities.

I don't expect you to agree with all the above. But do you agree that the issue described in paragraph one is an important one and that there is no easy way to settle it? . . .

Cordially yours,
RODERICK M. CHISHOLM

cases—and the program of this school is to start with these basic cases and understand reference in other cases as derivative in some way from these) is determined by the way the term, or rather the speaker's or the community's use of the term, is causally linked to external things. The word *cat* refers to cats because cats have figured (in a certain "appropriate" way) in interactions which have led us to use the word *cat* as we do. "Reference is a matter of causal chains of the appropriate type" might be the slogan of this group.

The problem these philosophers face (and as a skeptic I would say it is an insuperable problem) is to say why and how a certain kind of causal connection between the characteristics of a thing and the use of a word brings it about that the word refers to that kind of thing, and to say what that certain kind of causal connection is without using any "semantical" word (any word which presupposes the notion of reference) in the characterization. Since studying the sort of causal connection in question involves looking at groups of speakers rather than individual speakers, a science that answered these questions would have to be a social psychology rather than an individual psychology; and since the causal connection involves real external things, things which are not in the heads of the speakers, it would not be a methodologically solipsist psychology, not even in a communitarian sense of *methodological solipsism* (a solipsism with a *we* instead of an *I*). Thus thinkers who take this causal theory of reference seriously would reject Fodor's demand that psychology must be methodologically solipsist. Notice that if reference is essential to minds and the causal theory is even partly on the right track, then what makes a mind a mind is, in large part, the way it is hooked up to an external environment—a striking shift away from the British empiricist perspective!

Aristotle and M.I.T.

A causal theory of the referential powers of the mind cannot remain at the level of talk about "causal chains of the appropriate type," however. To persist there is not just to be guilty of vagueness, but to rely on an ancient (in fact, an Aristotelian) notion of efficient causation which is no more clear than reference itself. When we say, for example, that our encounters with cats are what have caused us to use the word *cat* as we do, we are relying on the old notion of cause-as-what-explains; what we mean is that events involving cats are what *explain* the fact that we use the word as we do. But to use an unreduced notion of explanation in a theory of reference would be to explain the obscure in terms of the more obscure.

To avoid such use of an unreduced notion of explanation while keeping the program will certainly be difficult. For a start, one might hope to eliminate vague talk of "the way we use the word '_____'" by actually constructing a model of the use of language. Some people say: "Well, we might somehow build a computer model—not just of the individual human but of the entire linguistic community in its environment. And when we get through with this huge model, it will somehow enable us to classify the causal chains that connect the subroutines inside the head of the speaker with external things and events." The only way one can think of doing this today is with the aid of the computer analogy; thus the M.I.T. program of a computer model of the "language organ," including a "semantic level of representation," would itself be one part of the larger program sketched by the causal theorists of reference. This would be a model of the use of language in a methodologically solipsist sense, the use insofar as it is contained inside the head of the individual speaker. In addition, of course, one would have somehow to classify the "causal chains" that connect these uses (subroutines inside the head of the speaker) with external things and events. The entire program might be called sociofunctionalism—the program, that is, of giving a model of the functional organization of a whole language-speaking community in its semantic relations to an environment.

This program hardly sounds more realistic than that other ancient program, the program of inductive logic: an algorithm which reproduces human scientific competence. But there is more wrong than just lack of realism. (After all, the devotees of this program would be content with progress in this direction; they do not seriously expect the entire program ever to be carried out, any more than—they would say—the entire program of physical science, the program of completely modelling the basic laws of nature, has to be carried out to justify physics as an activity.)

The difficulty is rather as follows. There *are* causal constraints on interpretation—we do expect some of the things speakers say to be "about" things they causally interact with, and we have some idea of the kind of causal interaction (for example, perceptual interaction) which is likely to be relevant. I interpret the speaker of a jungle language when I look at what he is seeing and touching and hearing, and I would assume that a lot of his words refer to the things he perceives.

But we do not always interpret speakers as if they were referring to whatever it is that caused them to introduce the word of locution they are using. How difficult interpretation can become! An example from the history of chemistry and metallurgy is instructive. In his great history of metallurgy, Cyril Smith has pointed out that the properties of the oxygen molecule do not really enter into the explanation of a number of the properties of metal calxes: what enters is rather the properties of the valence electrons of the metal itself. He once jokingly expressed this by saying, "Phlogiston *does* exist; it's valence electrons!" We don't say that, however. We say instead, "That's a nice joke but there really isn't any such substance as phlogiston."

The question I want to ask is, "Why isn't this true? *Why* doesn't *phlogiston* denote valence electrons?" The simple answer would be that the causal chain connecting valence electrons to the properties of calxes and thence, via human perception of those properties, to (the invention of phlogiston theory and) the use of the word *phlogiston* isn't "of the appropriate type." But isn't this the typical kind of causal chain in the case of a theoretical term in physics? An entity is responsible for the observable behavior of something or other, and observation of that behavior leads to the introduction of a theory containing a term which refers to that entity—refers to it even though typically we didn't get the properties of that entity exactly right when we first made up the theory (Putnam 1975b).

Another less simple answer—a better one—is that the causal chain is there, all right, but interpreting *phlogiston* as denoting valence electrons would falsify central beliefs of the people who used the term (as they thought) referentially. But look! Taking the word *electron*, as Bohr used it in 1900, to refer to electrons *also falsifies central beliefs of the people, including Bohr himself, who used it "referentially."* Bohr believed in 1900 that electrons had trajectories—had both position and momentum all the time. So he had centrally false beliefs about electrons. Yet we regard it as reasonable, nonetheless, to interpret his 1900 word *electron* as referring to what we now call electrons. And so did Bohr. By keeping the same word when he developed quantum mechanics, he treated his own sequence of theories as a sequence of better and better theories about the same things. (In Husserlian language, he treated electrons as an "ideal pole," a kind of ideal object about which we get convergent knowledge, even though what we say about them at any given time is not exactly right.)

This illustrates that causal constraints on reference have to be balanced against other constraints in the actual practice of interpretation. Interpreting someone is not something you can reduce to an algorithm. You can't do it by just looking at what he perceives, or looking at the phenomena he is trying to explain, or looking at all of this plus his beliefs, or rank-ordering his beliefs in terms of which are more or less central. We do manage to interpret one another; otherwise hermeneutics would be impossible and conversation would be impossible. But it takes all of the intelligence we have to do it.

To say what is an "appropriate kind of causal chain" we would have to have a *normative* theory of interpretation as a whole, not just a description of certain kinds of "causal chains." For interpretation (like theory formation in empirical science) is a holistic matter. What I'm leading up to is the *holism of interpretation*. In truth, a survey of interpretative rationality is as Utopian a project as a survey of scientific rationality.

There is one last element, and again I'm giving the case for Kantian pessimism. To ask what someone's—say, Jones's—words are about, how to interpret them, is a *normative* question. The question should not be confused with the question of what Jones would *say* his words are about, because very often speakers give terrible answers, as anyone in the field of linguistics knows. (When you ask explicit semantical questions, as linguists know who have worked with native informants, the first rule is not to let them know what you want to find out. For once the informant knows what you want to learn, you'll get ruined data. People will tell you, "Yes, we talk this way and not that way," and it will be absolutely wrong.)

Nor is Fodor's project—the project of saying what words have the same "content" and what words have different "content" without looking at the causal chains connecting those words to the external world—any better off (Putnam 1984). To attempt this is just to engage in theory of interpretation while throwing away a large part of the data (the data about the external correlates of the representations being processed by the brain); this won't make the task easier—rather it will make it impossible! But what if the task *is* impossible? The task of physics, as we said before, may also be impossible to fulfill, yet we are content, and rightly so, with partial success. Could not the "sociofunctionalist" view be correct in principle even if it cannot be carried out in practice?

For a long time this is what I myself believed (Putnam 1975c). But it now seems to me that there is an important difference between the two cases. What is analogous to the task of physics, perhaps, is the task of describing how the human brain actually works (either at a neurological or at a computational level). Progress certainly has been made in doing this—as an example of exciting work using computational models one thinks of the work of the late David Marr (Marr 1982). But the task of giving a computational analysis of meaning or reference seems to resemble this task less than it resembles the task of formalizing scientific reasoning (inductive logic). These latter two tasks—formalizing interpretation and formalizing nondemonstrative reasoning—are normative, or partly normative, in a way in which simply modelling how we actually see or think or interpret is not.

A correct model of how the brain works might, in the Utopian limit, actually predict what people will say about what a word refers to and about whether a phrase is or is not a good paraphrase of a given expression as used in a particular context. But if the question is not "Do most people think that *phlogiston* refers to valence electrons?" but is instead, "*Does phlogiston* refer to valence electrons?"; or if the question is not, "Do most people think that the phrase 'justifiably believes, what is in fact true, that . . .' is a reasonable paraphrase of the verbal phrase 'knows that . . .'?" but is instead, "*Is* 'justifiably believes, what is in fact true, that . . .' a *correct* paraphrase of the verbal phrase 'knows that . . .'?"; then, as I said before, we are asking a normative question. We are asking for an algorithmic or computer version of a normative account of interpretative rationality; and I, for one, see no reason to think this is possible. Indeed, if (as I believe) human interpretative rationality is deeply interwoven with human rationality in general, then constructing an algorithmic model of interpretation would presuppose constructing an algorithmic model of prescriptive rationality in general—and this is surely impossible for human minds to do, for Gödelian reasons among others (Putnam 1985b).

To close, we are back with the question Kant raised: the question, in contemporary rather than Kantian terms, whether the nature of semantical characteristics of representations is a problem for descriptive science at all. One great twentieth-century philosopher who would have answered "no" to this question—and not because he thought the question was answered by the work of Alfred Tarski—was Ludwig Wittgenstein. But his philosophy is both too complex and too close to my own time for me to attempt to survey here.

Perhaps it is enough if I have succeeded in indicating that the question of those "dualities in our experience" which don't seem to go away is still very much with us. If there is one value which a historical survey of what has been thought on these matters can have, it is to caution us against thinking that it is obvious even what the questions are. For part of what we have seen in this survey is that each previous period in the history of Western thought had a quite different idea of what such a term as *mind* or *soul* might stand for, and a correspondingly different idea of what the puzzles were that we should be trying to solve.

References

Aquinas, T. 1965. *On Being and Essence*. Translation and Interpretation by Joseph Bobik. Notre Dame: University of Notre Dame Press.

Berkeley, G. 1982. *A Treatise Concerning the Principles of Human Knowledge*. Edited by K. Winkler. Indianapolis: Hackett.

Boden, M. 1981. *Minds and Mechanisms: Philosophical Psychology and Computational Models*. Ithaca, N.Y.: Cornell University Press.

Chisholm, R. and Sellars, W. 1958. "Correspondence on Intentionality." In *Minnesota Studies in the Philosophy of Science, Vol. II, Concepts, Theories and the Mind-Body Problem*, pp. 521–539. Edited by H. Feigl, M. Scriven, and G. Maxwell. Minneapolis: University of Minnesota.

Fodor, J. 1975. *The Language of Thought*. New York: T. Y. Crowell.

Hoffman, P. 1985. "Descartes on the Ontological Status of Sensations." Unpublished.

Hume, D. 1978. *A Treatise of Human Nature*. 2nd ed. Edited by B. A. Selby-Bigge. New York: Oxford University Press.

Marr, D. 1982. *Vision: A Computational Investigation into the Human Representation and Processing of Visual Information*. San Francisco: W. H. Freeman.

Nussbaum, M. 1978. "The Role of *Phantasia* in Aristotle's Explanation of Action." In *Aristotle's De Motu Animalum*, pp. 221–270. Princeton, N.J.: Princeton University Press.

Putnam, H. 1975a. *Philosophical Papers, Vol. 1: Mathematics, Matter and Method*. New York: Cambridge University Press.

———. 1975b. "Explanation and Reference" and "Language and Reality." *Philosophical Papers, Vol. 2: Mind, Language and Reality*. New York: Cambridge University Press.

———. 1975c. "The Nature of Mental States" and "Philosophy and Our Mental Life." *Philosophical Papers, Vol. 2: Mind, Language and Reality*. New York: Cambridge University Press.

———. 1984. "Models and Modules." *Cognition* 17:253–264.

———. 1985a. "A Comparison of Something with Something Else." *New Literary History*. In press.

———. 1985b. "Reflexive Reflections." *Epistemology, Metaphysics and Philosophy of Science. Essays in Honour of Carl G. Hempel on the Occasion of His Eightieth Birthday, Jan. 8th, 1985*. Edited by W. K. Essler, H. Putnam, and W. Stegmüller. Dordrecht: Reidel.

Quine, W. 1981. *Theories and Things*. Cambridge, Mass.: Harvard University Press.

Sellars, W. 1963. "Empiricism and Abstract Entities." *The Philosophy of Rudolf Carnap*. Edited by Paul Schillp. LaSalle, Ill.: Open Court.

Strauss, L. 1963. *Moses ben Maimon: Guide to the Perplexed*. Translated by Shlomo Pines. Chicago: University of Chicago Press.

How Old Is Consciousness?

Julian Jaynes

I have noted with anticipatory interest that the title of Professor Putnam's essay is "How Old Is the Mind?" So in parallel fashion, I shall title my essay "How Old Is Consciousness?" for I think you will see that that is the substance of what, after several preliminaries, I shall present.

How old *is* consciousness? It is a question which, if it had been asked by a graduate student in psychology here at Iowa forty years ago, would have opened an urgent door for him to leave the university at the first possible moment. Such questions might contaminate the purity of behaviorism with its supposed groundings in logical positivism. Bergmann and Spence here at Iowa, along with Stevens and Boring at Harvard at about the same time, were promoting the idea of operational definitions to enable psychology to reach out and touch the other sciences in a movement called The Unity of Science. But operationism, even at that very time, was being cast off by physicists themselves. It contained logical contradictions (for example, a "thing" measured or observed in two ways is really two things) and regressions (for example, how do we operationally define the operationally defining measuring instruments?). Moreover, such a program, mistakenly insisting that all sciences travel the same route (Jaynes 1966), meant that the traditionally central problems of psychology were being smothered out of sight because they could not be operationally defined, namely consciousness and all that we associate with the term, our capacity to think of ourselves doing something we are not doing or being somewhere other than where we are, our easy ability to remember things in the past with its sense of time stretched out like a space behind us, as well as in front of us, all our fantasy and imagination—so different from the behaviorist concept of habit—and all our experiences in those narratives during REM sleep that we call dreams. All of this basic central material of psychology, so apparent and exciting and interesting to the growing child, all was banished from scientific consideration. It is truly an astonishing phenomenon in intellectual history that the very heart of the study of minds could under the scientific politics and fashions of the middle of the twentieth century so easily be pushed out of sight. And we are really not out of that period yet.

Now, in the immediate aftermath of behaviorism and logical positivism has come cognitive psychology, which is sometimes—but not always—still in the great stubborn shadow of behaviorism. Its central position seems to me familiar as old fashioned stimulus-response psychology but with something called "representations" in between, representations which can be either propositional or iconic. (For a criticism of "representations," see Jaynes, 1982.) Rarely with this paradigm do or can cognitive psychologists refer to consciousness, or even need to; rarely do they pay attention to introspection or imagination. And even more rarely do we find a cognitive psychologist looking at the problem from the point of view of the first two sessions of this conference, that of its origin in evolution, experience, or history. And out of such refusal to ask the important diachronic questions has come the ease with which cognitive psychologists—as well as those philosophers called functionalists, of whom I believe Professor Putnam was once one—the ease with which some of them have taken up the computer as a model of mind. This is again to me a retreat from the direct study of consciousness. So much for this curious historical avoidance of both the term and the group of abilities it refers to.

So, how old is consciousness? Let us first be clear about what it is we are talking about. Perhaps the simplest possible definition is that consciousness pertains to that which the average person would answer to the question "What are you thinking about?" I say average person, because the sophisticated intellectual who has thought about this problem is so full of adversarial theories and past errors about consciousness that he might find it difficult, if not contrary to some previous intellectual allegiance, to honestly reply. But this is the best denotative or ostensive definition (in contrast to a connotative definitive which I will come to in a moment) that can be suggested. Denotative definitions are pointing at the thing to be defined. Take any ten people on the street right now in Iowa City and ask them that question: What are you thinking about? These are the data referred to by the term consciousness. I am not saying that all consciousness is introspection, but rather that it is introspectible (what we have access to in our "minds," a definition in absolute agreement with Descartes, Locke, Hume, and the tradition that followed).

I have just mentioned that many sophisticated people find such a simplicity disagreeable because they have been filled with past errors about consciousness, errors that have indeed been committed by the intellectual community. Consciousness came to be confused with sense perception by philosophers such as Russell or G. E. Moore, and also in the psychophysics of Fechner and the experimentalism of Wundt. The elements one could analyze out of a perception were the elements of consciousness. How strange and foreign that would be to our ten subjects out on the street this morning! You would not find them describing to you bundles of sense-perceptions or just noticeable differences, but rather a stream of worries, regrets, hopes, reminiscences, interior dialogues and monologues, plans, imaginations—all of which are the stuff of consciousness.

And if any of you still thinks that sense perception is to be equated with consciousness, then I think you can follow a path to a reductio ad absurdum: you would then have to say that since all animals have sense perception, all are conscious, and so on, back through the evolutionary tree even to one-celled protozoa, and thence even to the amoeboid white cells of the blood, since they sense bacteria and devour them. They too, then, would be conscious. And to say that there are ten thousand conscious beings per cubic millimeter of blood whirling around in the circulatory systems of each of us is a position few would wish to defend. You must separate consciousness from perception.

Now while sense perception is not due to consciousness, we are of course conscious of what we perceive. But there are many experiments and phenomena which demonstrate that perception can occur without consciousness.

Another error is that consciousness makes copies of experience. That consciousness does not copy experience can be shown very easily in two ways: by examining the absence of memories that we should have if consciousness did copy experience (for example, we would then all know at once what letters correspond to what numbers on telephones, but most of us don't); or by examining the memories we have and noting that they are not structured like their associated experiences (for example, think of the last time you were swimming; most people, instead of envisioning the complicated visual, thermal, proprioceptive and respiratory experience that it actually was, tend to see themselves swimming from another point of view—a bird's-eye view perhaps—something they have never experienced at all).

A further error is that consciousness is necessary for learning—the mistake I labored under for so long. But many experiments in psychology demonstrate that learning, be it conditioning, motor learning, or instrumental learning, can go on without consciousness. This is not to say that consciousness does not play a role in these different types of human learning. It does, as in decisions as to what to learn, or the making of rules for improving learning, or the conscious verbalizing of aspects of a task. But this is not the learning itself. And my point is that consciousness is not necessary for learning to occur.

One could here bring up the well-known phenomenon of the automatization of habit, for when this happens to us, it seems that the task has required consciousness at the beginning, but as the habit is perfected consciousness eases away and the task is performed effortlessly. This same smoothing out and increased rapidity of a habit with practice is universal among animals that learn. Generally, in this ubiquitous phenomenon, it is not necessarily or basically the lapsing of consciousness with improved performance so much as the lapsing of forced attention to components of the task. And attention, external attention, which is the focusing of sense perception, is not necessarily conscious. To take two coins in either hand, and toss them across each other so that the opposite hand catches each, is a task that will take somewhere between fifteen and twenty trials to learn. And if you wish to try it this evening and monitor your consciousness while you are doing so, you will find that consciousness has little to do with the learning that seems to go on mechanically. You might be conscious of something about your clumsiness, or the silliness of what you are doing as you keep picking the coins up from the floor, until, at the point of success, your consciousness is somewhat surprised and even proud of your superior dexterity. It is the attention which has changed. Automatization is a diminution of attention, not consciousness.

Consciousness is also not necessary for judgments, reasoning, and problem solving. That it is not needed may seem rather paradoxical and concerns one of the forgotten experiments of psychology. It is indeed so simple to us nowadays that it seems silly. And yet to me it's as important in the history of psychology as the very complicated Michelson-Morley experiment was in the history of physics (Swenson 1972). As the latter showed that the aether did not exist, setting the stage for relativity theory, so the experiment I am about to describe showed that thinking was not conscious, setting the stage for the kind of theorizing I am describing here.

The experiment I refer to was first performed in 1901 by Karl Marbe, a graduate student at Würzburg (Marbe 1901), back in a scientific world where consciousness was being intensively studied for the first time. Using his professors as subjects, each of whom had had the experience of one thousand previous experiments in introspection, he asked them to make a simple judgment between two identical-looking weights as to which was the heavier. Against the background of the experimental psychology of the time, the result was astonishing. There was no conscious content for the actual judgment itself, although such a judgment was embedded in the consciousness of the problem, its materials, and technique.

So began what came to be called the Würzburg School of Imageless Thought, which led through experiments by Ach, Watt, Kulpe, and others to concepts such as set, *aufgabe*, and determining tendency—which I have renamed structions. Structions are like instructions given to the nervous system, which, when presented with the materials to work on, arrives at the answer automatically without any conscious thinking or reasoning. And this phenomenon applies to most of our activities, all the way from such simplicities as judging weights, to solving problems, to scientific and philosophical activity. Consciousness studies a problem and prepares it as a struction, a process which may result in a sudden appearance of the solution as if out of nowhere. During World War II, British physicists used to say that they no longer made their discoveries in the laboratory; they had three *B*'s where their discoveries were made: the bath, the bed, and the bus. And as I have mentioned earlier, this process on a smaller scale is going on in me at present, as my words are "as if chosen for me" by my nervous system after giving it the struction of my intended meaning.

Finally, in this list of mistakes about consciousness, a word about its location. Most people who have thought long about the problem and so placed consciousness "out there" in the intellectual domain, tend to think of their consciousness—much as Descartes, Locke, and Hume did—as a space usually located inside their heads. Particularly when we make eye contact, we tend to—in a subliminal way—infer such space in others. There is of course no such space whatever. The space of consciousness, which I shall hereafter call mind-space, is a functional space that has no location except as we assign one to it. To think of our consciousness as inside our heads is, because of all our words like *introspection* and *internalization,* a very natural but arbitrary thing to do. I certainly don't mean to say that consciousness is separate from the brain; by the assumptions of natural science, it is not. But we use our brains in riding bicycles, and yet no one considers that the location of bicycle riding is inside our heads. The phenomenal location of consciousness is arbitrary.

To sum up so far, we have shown that consciousness is not all mentality, not necessary for sensation or perception, that it is not a copy of experience, nor necessary for learning, nor even necessary for thinking and reasoning, and that it has only an arbitrary and functional location. As a prelude to what I am to say later, I wish you to consider that there could have been at one time human beings who did most of the things we do—speak, understand, perceive, solve problems, and so on—but who were without consciousness. I think this is a very important possibility.

So far this is almost going back to a radical behaviorist position. But what then is consciousness, since I regard it as an irreducible fact that my introspections are as real as so-called external perceptions, though with a distinguishingly incongruent quality? My procedure here will be to outline in somewhat terse fashion a theory of consciousness and then to explain it in various ways.

What Consciousness Is

Subjective conscious mind is an analog of what we call the real world. It is built up with a vocabulary or lexical field whose terms are all metaphors or analogs of behavior in the physical world. Its reality is of the same order as mathematics. It allows us to short-cut behavioral processes and arrive at more adequate decisions. Like mathematics, it is an operator rather than a thing or a repository. And it is intimately bound up with volition and decision.

Consider the language we use to describe conscious processes. The most prominent group of words used to describe mental events are visual. We 'see' solutions to problems, the best of which may be 'brilliant' or 'clear' or possibly 'dull', 'fuzzy', 'obscure'. These words are all metaphors, and the mind-space to which they apply is generated by metaphors of actual space (and I indicate this by using single quotation marks). In that space we can 'approach' a problem, perhaps from some 'viewpoint', and 'grapple' with its difficulties. Every word we use to refer to mental events is a metaphor or analog of something in the behavioral world. And the adjectives that we use to describe physical behavior in real space are analogically taken over to describe mental behavior in mind-space. We speak of the conscious mind as being 'quick' or 'slow', or of somebody being 'nimble-witted' or 'strong-minded' or 'weak-minded' or 'broad-minded' or 'deep' or 'open' or 'narrow-minded'. And so, as in a real space, something can be at the 'back' of our minds or in the 'inner-recesses' or 'beyond' our minds. But, someone might say, metaphor is a mere comparison and cannot make new entities like consciousness. A proper analysis of metaphor shows quite the opposite. In every metaphor there are at least two terms, the thing we are trying to express in words, the *metaphrand*, and the term produced by a struction to do so, the *metaphier*. These are similar to what I. A. Richards called the tenor and the vehicle, terms more suitable to poetry than to psychological analysis (Richards 1936). I have chosen *metaphrand* and *metaphier* instead to have more of the connotation of an operator by echoing the arithmetic terms *multiplicand* and *multiplier*. If I say the ship plows the sea, the metaphrand is the way the bow goes through the water and the metaphier is a plow.

As a more relevant example, suppose we are a person back at the formation of our mental vocabulary, and we have been trying to solve some problem or to learn how to perform some task. To express our success, we might suddenly exclaim, "Aha! I 'see' the solution." 'See' is the metaphier, drawn from the physical behavior from the physical world, that is applied to this otherwise inexpressible mental occurrence, the metaphrand. But metaphiers usually have associations that we are calling *paraphiers*, which then project back into the metaphrand as what are called *paraphrands* and, indeed, create new entities. The word 'see' has associations of seeing in the physical world and therefore of space, and this space then becomes a paraphrand as it is united with this inferred mental event called the metaphrand.

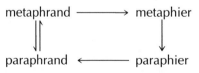

In this way the spatial quality of the world around us is being driven into the psychological fact of solving a problem (which, as we remember, needs no consciousness). And as a result of the language we use to describe such psychological events, this associated spatial quality becomes with constant repetitions the spatial quality of our consciousness, or mind-space. This mind-space I regard as the primary feature of consciousness. It is the space which, because of my suggestion, you are introspecting on at this very moment.

But who does the 'seeing'? Who does the introspecting? Here we introduce analogy, which differs from metaphor in that the similarity is between relationships rather than between things or sections. As the body with its sense organs (referred to as *I*) is to physical seeing, so there develops automatically an *analog 'I'* to relate to this mental kind of 'seeing' in mind-space. The analog 'I' is the second most important feature of consciousness. It is not to be confused with the self, which is an object of consciousness in later development. The analog 'I' is contentless, related I think to Kant's transcendental ego. As the bodily I can move about in its environment looking at this or that, so the analog 'I' learns to 'move about' in mind-space concentrating on one thing or another. If you 'saw' yourself swimming in our earlier example, it was your analog 'I' that was doing the 'seeing'.

A third feature of consciousness we are calling *narratization*, the analogic simulation of actual behavior, an obvious aspect of consciousness which seems to have escaped previous synchronic discussions of consciousness. Consciousness is constantly fitting things into a story, putting a before and an after around any event. This feature is an analog of our physical selves moving about through a physical world with its spatial successiveness which becomes the successiveness of time in mind-space. And this results in the conscious conception of time as a *spatialized time* in which we locate events and indeed our lives. It is impossible to be conscious of time in any other way than as a space.

There are other features of consciousness which I shall simply mention: *concentration*, the 'inner' analog of external perceptual attention; *suppression*, by which we stop being conscious of annoying thoughts, the analog of turning away from annoyances in the physical world; *excerption*, the analog of how we sense only one aspect of a thing at a time; and *consilience*, the analog of perceptual assimilation; and there are others. In no way is my list meant to be exhaustive. The essential rule here is that no operation goes on in consciousness that was not in behavior first. All of these are learned analogs of external behavior.

Psychologists are sometimes justly accused of the habit of reinventing the wheel and making it square and then calling it a first approximation. I would demur from agreeing that this is true in the development I have just outlined, but I would indeed like to call it a first approximation. Consciousness is not a simple matter and it should not be spoken of as if it were. Nor have I mentioned the different *modes of narratization* in consciousness, such as the verbal, perceptual, bodily, or musical modes, all of which seem quite distinct with properties of their own. But it is enough, I think, to allow us to go back to the evolutionary problem as I stated it in the beginning, a problem that has caused so much trouble in biology, psychology, and philosophy.

When did all this 'inner' world begin? Here we arrive at the most important watershed in our discussion. Saying that consciousness is developed out of language means that everybody from Darwin right on, including myself in my earlier years, was absolutely wrong in trying to trace out the origin of consciousness biologically or neurophysiologically. It means we have to look at human history after language evolved and ask when in history an analog 'I' narratizing in a mind-space began.

When did language evolve? Elsewhere (Jaynes 1976b) I have outlined ideas of how language could have evolved from call modification; this has been called the "Wahee, Wahoo" model and is at present in competition with several others (Maxwell 1984). But such theorizing points to the late Pleistocene or Neanderthal Era on several grounds: (1) such a period coincides with an evolutionary pressure over the last glacial period for verbal communication in the hunting of large animals; (2) it coincides with the astonishing development of the particular areas of the brain involved in language; and, (3) what is unique in this theory, it corresponds to the archeological record of an explosion of tool artifacts, for we know that language is not just communication but also an organ of perception, directing attention and holding attention on a particular object or task, making advanced tool making possible. This dating means that language is no older than fifty thousand years, which means that consciousness developed sometime between that date and the present.

It is fortunate for this problem that by 3000 B.C., human beings had learned the remarkable ability of writing. It is therefore obvious that our first step should be to look at the early writings of mankind to see if there is evidence of an analog 'I' narratizing in a mind-space. The first writing is in hieroglyphics and cuneiform, both very difficult to translate, especially when they refer to anything psychological. Therefore we should go to a language with which we have some continuity, such

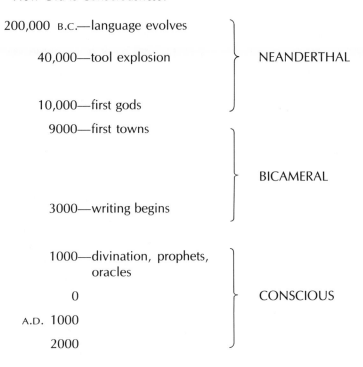

200,000 B.C.—language evolves

40,000—tool explosion   NEANDERTHAL

10,000—first gods

9000—first towns

     BICAMERAL

3000—writing begins

1000—divination, prophets,
           oracles

0   CONSCIOUS

A.D. 1000

2000

as Greek. The earliest Greek writing of sufficient size to test our question is *The Iliad*. Are the characters in *The Iliad* narratizing with an analog 'I' in a mind-space and making decisions in this way?

The Bicameral Mind

First, let me make a few generalizations about *The Iliad*. To me and to roughly half of the classicists, it is oral poetry, originally spoken and composed at the same time by a long succession of *aoidoi* or bards. As such, it contained many incongruities even after it was written down, perhaps by someone named Homer; it had many interpolations added to it. So there are many exceptions to what I am about to say, such as the long speech of Nestor in Book 11, or Achilles' rhetorical reply to Odysseus in Book 9. But if you take the generally accepted oldest parts of *The Iliad* and ask whether there is evidence of consciousness, the answer, I think, is no. People are not sitting down and making decisions. No one is. No one is introspecting. No one is even reminiscing. It's a very different kind of world.

Then who makes the decisions? Whenever a significant choice is to be made, a voice comes in telling people what to do. These voices are always and immediately obeyed. Those voices are called gods. To me this is the origin of gods. I regard them as auditory hallucinations similar to, although not precisely the same as, the voices that Joan of Arc or William Blake heard. Or similar to the voices that modern schizophrenics hear. Similar perhaps to the voices that some of you here in this room have heard, while it is a very significant item of the DSM III—DSM = Diagnostic and Statistical Manual (American Psychiatric Association 1980)—for schizophrenia. Auditory hallucinations also occur in some form at some time in about half the general population (Posey and Losch 1983). I have also corresponded with or met people who are completely normal in function but who suddenly have a period of hearing extensive verbal hallucinations, usually of a religious sort. Verbal hallucinations are common today, but back in early civilization, I suggest, they were universal.

This mentality in early times, as in *The Iliad*, is what we call the *bicameral mind*, on the metaphier of a bicameral legislature. It simply means that human mentality at this time was in two parts, a decision-making part and a follower part, and neither part was conscious in the sense in which I have described consciousness. I would like to remind you here of the critique of consciousness with which I began my talk, which demonstrated that human beings could speak and understand, solve problems, and do much that we do but without being conscious. So could bicameral man. In his everyday life he was a creature of habit, but when there arose some kind of problem that needed a new decision, stress was enough to instigate an auditory hallucination, which, because such individuals had no mind-space in which to question or rebel, had to be obeyed.

But why is there such a mentality as a bicameral mind? Let us go back to the beginning of civilization in several sites in the Near East around 9000 B.C. The bicameral mind is concomitant with the beginning of agriculture-based towns or cities. In such circumstances a bicameral mentality would enable a large group to carry around with them the directions of the chief or king as verbal hallucinations, instead of the chieftain having to be present at all times. I think that verbal hallucinations had evolved along with language during the Neanderthal Era as aids to attention and perseverance in tasks, but then became the way of ruling larger groups.

It can easily be inferred that human beings with such a mentality had to exist in a special kind of society, one rigidly ordered in strict hierarchies with strict expectancies organized into the mind, so that such hallucinations preserved the social fabric. And such was definitely the case. Bicameral kingdoms were all hierarchical theocracies, with a god, often an idol, at its head from whom hallucinations seemed to come, or more rarely with a human being who was divine and whose actual voice was heard in hallucinations.

Such civilizations started in various sites in the Near East and spread into Egypt. Later they spread from Egypt into the Kush in southern Sudan and then into central Africa, and in the other direction into Anatolia, Crete, Greece, and then into India and southern Russia. They then spread into the Malay Peninsula, where the ruins of another civilization have just been discovered in northern Thailand, and then later into China. A millennium later such a series of civilizations appeared in Mesoamerica and led up to the Aztec civilization, and then—partly independently and partly by diffusion—led to a series of civilizations in the Andean highlands culminating in the Inca. Wherever we look there is some kind of evidence of what I am calling the bicameral mind. Every ancient historian would agree that all of these early civilizations were thoroughly religious, heavily dependent on gods and idols.

Where we have writing after 3000 B.C., we can see these bicameral civilizations much more clearly. In Mesopotamia the head of state was a wooden statue—wooden so it could be carried about—with jewels in its eyes. It was perfumed, richly raimented, centered in ritual, and seated behind a large table (the origin of our altars) in the gigunu, which was a large hall in the bottom of a ziggurat. What we might call the king was really the first steward of this statue god. Cuneiform texts literally describe how people came to the idol-statues, asked them questions, and received directions from them.

This kind of hearing from idols was everywhere in bicameral civilizations, and I was very troubled when I went back to The Iliad, where I got the idea of the bicameral mind, and found no idols at all. So I went to Athens and talked with the Curator of Antiquities at the National Museum and asked him if he had noticed that there were no idols in The Iliad. He replied that he hadn't, but that it was curious, because excavated temples from that period of the Trojan War, namely around 1200 B.C., have been full of broken idols. In other words, all the idols have been expunged from The Iliad as it has come down to us, just as have most of the idols in the Hebrew Testament. Just why the minds (or brains) of bicameral people needed such external props as idols for their voices is difficult to answer, but I suspect it had to do with the necessary visual differentiation of one god from another. I should also mention that the evidence suggests that everyone had a personal god. In Mesopotamia, it was the person's *ili*, a word which comes perhaps from the same root as the Hebrew Eli and Elohim. In Egypt, the personal god was the *ka*, and it had the same function as the *ili*. Until recently, the word *ka* had been an enigma in Egyptology.

In connection with the personal god, it is possible to suggest that a part of our innate bicameral heritage is the modern phenomenon of the 'imaginary' playmate. It occurs in one-third of modern children between the ages of two and five, and is believed now to involve very real verbal hallucinations. In the rare cases where the imaginary playmate lasts beyond the juvenile period, it grows up with the child and begins telling him or her what to do in times of stress. It is therefore possible that this is how personal gods started in bicameral times, growing up with the person in a society of expectancies that constantly encouraged the child to hear voices.

This, then, is the bicameral mind. I have not had the time to discuss the various bicameral theocracies, but all were based on strict and stable hierarchies, as I have stressed more fully elsewhere (Jaynes 1976a). At least some of these civilizations could be compared to nests of social insects, where instead of the social control being exerted by pheromones from a queen insect, it was exerted through hallucinatory directions from an idol. Everything went like clockwork, provided there was no real catastrophe or problem.

The Breakdown of the Bicameral Mind

But such a system is obviously precarious. The huge success of such agricultural bicameral civilizations inevitably leads to overpopulation and complexity, and given a time of social and political instability, bicamerality can break down like a house of cards. Some civilizations broke down frequently, like the Mayans on this continent. A temple complex and city would be built up, last a few centuries and then be completely abandoned, presumably because as the society became more and more populous, the voices didn't agree anymore. And then after living a few centuries as tribal bands, the people would somehow get together again and another temple complex would be built up. This is why so many of these temple complexes show evidence of people just leaving them enmasse when presumably the voices did not work.

In Egypt we find that the bicameral mind broke down between what is called the Old Kingdom and what is called the Middle Kingdom, and then again between the Middle Kingdom and the New Kingdom. The evidence for these dark, chaotic periods appears in the hieroglyphic writings.

But in Mesopotamia, which was the most stable society in the world, there does not seem to have been a breakdown until around 1400 B.C. The graphics of the period no longer depict gods. In some instances kings beg in front of empty gods' thrones—nothing like that had ever occurred before. Another line of evidence is in the cuneiform literature. In *The Epic of Tijulti-Ninurta*, for the first time in history gods are spoken of as forsaking human beings. The greatest literature of the period, possibly the origin of the Book of Job, is the *Ludlul Bel Nemequi*, the first readable lines of which translate as:

> My god has forsaken me and disappeared,
> My goddess has failed me and keeps at a distance,
> The good angel who walked beside me has departed.

How similar to some of our Hebrew psalms—Psalm 42, for example.

The reasons for this breakdown are several. The success of bicameral civilization leads to overpopulation—as I have mentioned, and this is described in texts from the period. There were various huge catastrophes, such as the Thera eruption, which I think most people know about now. It is the origin of Plato's myth of Atlantis. The ensuing tsunami (tidal wave) crushed all the bicameral kingdoms around that part of the Mediterranean, resulting in large migrations of people looking for "promised lands," looking for a place to settle down with their gods again and start another bicameral civilization. One of the reasons that we still have problems in that area of the world, I think, goes right back to this chaotic time. Another cause is writing itself, because once something is written you can turn away from it and it has no more power over you, in contrast to an auditory hallucination, which you cannot shut out. Writing, particularly as used extensively in Hammurabi's hegemony, weakened the power of the auditory directions. This, and the complexities of overpopulation and the complexities of huge migrations as one population moved in on others, these are the obvious causes. And in this breakdown, various things start to happen, including, I think, the beginning of consciousness.

The immediate results of this breakdown are several and new in world history. The idea of heaven as where the gods have gone, the idea of genii or angels as messengers between heaven and earth, the idea of evil gods such as demons—all are new phenomena. By 1000 B.C. people in Babylon were walking around draped with amulets which we find archeologically by the thousands. They wore these to protect themselves from a huge variety of demons.

The Beginning of Consciousness

And then, far more interestingly, came the development of a new way of making decisions, a kind of proto-consciousness. All significant decisions previously had been based on the bicameral mind. But after its breakdown, after the hallucinated voices no longer told people what to do, various ways of discerning messages from the gods and making decisions developed. We call these methods divination. Throwing lots was the simplest kind. But putting oil on water; throwing dice; studying the movements of smoke; a priest whispering a prayer into a sacrificial animal, sacrificing it, and then looking at its internal organs to find out what the god intends—all of these were extensively and officially practiced. And then there was the method of divination that is still around, astrology. It is remarkable to go back and read the cuneiform letters of kings to their astrologers and diviners from around 1000 B.C. These cruel Assyrian tyrants, who are depicted in their bas-reliefs as grappling with lions and engaging in fierce animal hunts, are, in their letters, meek and frightened people. They don't know what to do. Astrologers tell them, "You cannot move out of your home for five days," "You must not eat this or that," "You should not wear clothes today"—extraordinary strictures that official diviners would say the gods meant. And not only has astrology lasted into our times, but it now has more followers than at any time previously in the entire history of the world.

In Greece just following the period I have been referring to in Mesopotamia, we can trace the bicameral mind as shown in the Linear B Tablets through *The Iliad* and *The Odyssey*, through the lyric and elegiac poetry of the next two centuries, as in Sappho and Archilochus, until we come to Solon in 600 B.C. Solon is the first person who said "Know thyself," although the saying is sometimes attributed to the Delphic Oracle. How can you know yourself unless you have an analog *I* narratizing in a mind-space and reminiscing or having episodic memory about what you have been doing and who you are? In Greece, then, we can see in detail the invention and learning of consciousness on the basis of metaphor by tracing out through these writings the change in words like *phrenes, kardia, psyche* (what I have called pre-conscious hypostases) from objective referents to mental functions.

The same kind of development in ancient China has been studied by a colleague of mine, Dr. Michael Carr of the University of Otaru. Comparing the four successive parts of the most ancient collection of texts, *The Shijing,* we find the same internalization process for such words as *Xin,* until they become the concept of mind or consciousness in China.

We can also see this rise of consciousness among the refugees from the Thera eruption that I mentioned. The word for refugees in Akkad, the ancient language of Babylon, is *khabiru,* which becomes our word Hebrew. And the story of the Hebrews, or really one branch of the Hebrews, is told in what we call the Hebrew Testament or the Old Testament.

Those of you who know biblical scholarship will know that the Hebrew Testament is a patchwork of writings put together around 600 B.C.—the date keeps coming forward. So using it as data is something of a problem. But there are several ways of entering this mosaic of much edited texts to test the theory, and here I shall mention only one. If we take the purer books, those that are all of one piece, singly authored, and that can be clearly and firmly dated, and compare the oldest with the most recent, such a comparison should reflect the differences in mentality we are referring to. The oldest of them is the Book of Amos, coming from about 800 B.C., and the most recent is the Book of Ecclesiastes, which comes at about 200 B.C.

Such prophets as Amos were leftover bicameral or semi-bicameral persons in the conscious era who heard and could relay the voice of Yahweh with a convincing authenticity, and who were therefore highly prized in their societies as reaching back to the lost bicameral kingdom. Amos is not a wise old man, but a shepherd boy, brought in from the fields of Tekoa, who hears the voice of Yahweh perhaps because he has been hearing it from other shepherds around him and stored it up as admonitory experience. Asked if he is a prophet, he doesn't even know what the word means. He says he isn't and then says, "Thus sayest the Lord," as the King James translates it, and out come some of the most powerful passages in Jewish history with such an authenticity that Amos is always surrounded by scribes taking down his words.

Ecclesiastes is just the opposite. The author begins by saying, "I *saw* in my heart that wisdom excelleth folly . . ."—a metaphoric use of 'see'. Spatialized time is something that I haven't dwelt upon, but which is one of the hallmarks of consciousness, because we cannot think of time apart from making a space out of it. This is very much in evidence in Ecclesiastes as, for example, in that oft quoted but still beautiful hymn to time that begins the third chapter: "For everything there is a season, and a time for every matter under heaven, a time to be born, and a time to die," and so on, with times like spaces for everything. Historically, we could then go further into the New Testament and note the even greater emphasis on conscious internalization.

Four Ideas

I can sum up what I have said so far as three major ideas about the origin of consciousness. The first idea is a theory of consciousness itself—that consciousness arises from the power of language to make metaphors and analogies. The second idea, which I didn't label as such, is the idea of the bicameral mind, an early type of mentality. I think the evidence for its existence is quite good. Apart from this idea, there is a problem of explaining the origin of gods, the origin of religion, and the huge, strange pageant of religious practices in these back corridors of time that we have good solid data for. The bicameral mind ties it all together and gives us a rationale for all of it. The third idea is that consciousness followed the bicameral mind. I have placed the date somewhere between 1400 B.C. and 600 B.C. This is a long period, and that date may have to be adjusted, but I believe this to be a good approximation.

However, a weak form of the theory could say no: consciousness goes all the way back to the beginning of language. After all, people could make metaphors back at the beginning of language—that is how language grew. Consciousness could have originated in exactly the same way back then, and then existed in parallel with the bicameral mind. Then the bicameral mind was sloughed off at the time I have suggested and consciousness came into its own. I do not choose to hold this weak theory because it is almost undisprovable. I think a hypothesis should be disprovable if we are going to call it a scientific hypothesis, and so I am sticking with the idea that consciousness followed the bicameral mind. Further, I don't see why you would have needed any consciousness if you did have the bicameral mind back then.

The fourth idea that I am going to end with is the neurological model for the bicameral mind. Since the bicameral mind was so important in history, responsible for civilization, what could have been going on in the brain? The proper strategy for trying to answer such a question is to take the simplest idea you can think of and then set about to disprove it. If you disprove it, go on to something more complicated.

The simplest idea is indeed the lateralized hemispheres. Could it be that in ancient peoples the right hemisphere was talking to the left, and that this was the bicameral mind? Could it be that control of speech usually resided in the speech areas of the left hemisphere in order to leave the corresponding areas of the right hemisphere free for the gods? That is a somewhat questionable way to say it, because there are other reasons for lateralization of function. But on the other hand, there is a kind of rationality here that I like. What *is* an auditory hallucination? Why was it so ubiquitous? Why was it present in civilizations all over the world?

If we assume that all admonitory information was being processed in the right hemisphere, and stored there until it needed to be accessed, how did such complicated processed admonitions get across the fewer fibres of the commissures to the left or dominant hemisphere? And particularly if, as I have supposed, the far fewer fibres of the anterior commissures that in humans connect the two temporal lobes were the ones involved? Such complicated transfer would be more efficiently handled if it was put into some kind of code. And what better code is there than human language? So, wouldn't it be interesting if indeed what might correspond to Wernicke's area in the right temporal lobe might be the area that was involved in storing up admonitory information, processing it in such a way that it produced answers to problems and decisions (which is what the bicameral mind is), and then using the code of language to get it across to the left hemisphere, the hemisphere that speaks, obeys, and manages behavior?

At the time I was thinking in this primitive fashion, in the early 1960s, there was little interest in the right hemisphere. Even as late as 1964, no less a scientist than J. Z. Young at the opening of the new Biology/Psychology Building at McGill said that the right hemisphere did nothing; it was simply a spare tire. But since then we have seen an explosion of findings about right-hemisphere function, leading, I am afraid, to a popularization that verges on some of the shrill excesses of similar discussions of asymmetrical hemisphere function in the latter part of the nineteenth century (Harrington, in press).

But the main results, even conservatively treated, generally agree with what we might expect to find in the right hemisphere on the basis of bicameral theory. The most significant such finding is that the right hemisphere is the synthetic hemisphere, fitting things together. Koh's block test is commonly used clinically to assess this ability and to test for right-hemisphere damage. Those who have seen the films of the first commissurotomy patient of Dr. Bogen, "W. J.," will remember his being given Koh's block test, and how quickly and deftly his left hand, using the right hemisphere, completed the block design. His performance seemed to be better than normal. And then when he used the right hand, which is operated by the left hemisphere (when of course he could no longer access his right hemisphere abilities because the commissures had been cut), it looked as if the right hand was teasing as it fumbled around and could not complete this simple task, even as the left hand tried to sneak up and help its task-incompetent partner. The chief function of the admonitory gods was indeed that of fitting people and functions into these societies. In other words, I think the gods would be very good at Koh's block test, and I am suggesting that much of the difference we can observe today between the hemispheres can be seen as echoing the differences between the two sides of the bicameral mind.

In summary, I would like to repeat these four ideas or modules of the theory I have presented. The first module includes the nature of consciousness, its origin in language (which can be studied in the learning of consciousness in children), and its changes in recent history. The second idea is that of the bicameral mind, which can be studied directly in ancient texts and indirectly in modern schizophrenia. Third is the idea that consciousness followed the bicameral mind, which can be studied in the artifacts and texts of history. And the fourth is that the neurological model for the bicameral mind is related to the two hemispheres. This can be studied in laterality differences today.

Well, to close with some remarks that echo my beginning, how old is consciousness? Three thousand years. And, what would the Iowa Department of Psychology of a half-century ago have thought of all this? No one, I venture, would have stayed to listen. Where are the measurements, where are the operational definitions? How could all this fit into the golden promise of The Unity of Science? Where are the reproducible, empirical experiments on which any natural science must be based? Where is the *experimentum crucis* by which we can decide if what I have said is true? Or is one conceivable?

The way to deal with such scorn is to bear it and to realize the falsity of the hardened stereotypes of natural science in the minds of behavioral scientists of fifty years ago. If adhered to, science could not even admit the theory of evolution by natural selection, since this theory too can have no clean, single experiment as proof of its validity. The theory of the origin of consciousness in the breakdown of the bicameral mind must seek other sources of support, a confluence of inductions, perhaps, from many different sources of evidence. We should, I think, be interested in the theory if it unifies and makes sense of a large set of phenomena, heretofore disjointed and unexplained. Such large and independent classes of facts include the narratizing nature of consciousness, which we know by introspection; the origin of beings called gods; the worldwide presence and power of religions; the nature of oracles and prophets at a particular time in history; the peculiarities of mind in schizophrenia as a partial vestige of the bicameral mind, or the malleability of mind in hypnosis (both topics I have dealt with elsewhere); and, what I have not had time to speak about here, the historically documented change in the nature of dreaming in the first millennium B.C., and the kind of data collected on the mentality of primitive people before their contacts with civilizations (see Levy-Bruhl 1926). If the principle—that consciousness developed during historical time out of an earlier nonconscious mentality—does explain these and other large bodies of facts, it ought to be provisionally accepted. And I think it does.

References

American Psychiatric Association. 1980. *Diagnostic and Statistical Manual*. 3rd ed. Washington, D.C.: American Psychiatric Association.

Harrington, A. In press. "Nineteenth Century Ideas on Hemisphere Differences and 'Duality of Mind'." *Behavioral and Brain Sciences*.

Jaynes, J. 1966. "The Routes of Science." *American Scientist* 54:94–102.

———. 1976a. *The Origin of Consciousness in the Breakdown of the Bicameral Mind*. Boston: Houghton Mifflin Co.

———. 1976b. "The Evolution of Language in the Late Pleistocene." *Annals of the New York Academy of Sciences* 28:312–325.

———. 1982. "Representations as Metaphiers." *Behavioral and Brain Sciences* 5:379–380.

Levy-Bruhl, L. 1926. *How Natives Think*. New York: Knopf.

Marbe, K. 1901. *Experimentell-Psychologische Untersuchungen über das Urteil*. Leipzig: Engelmann.

Maxwell, M. 1984. *Human Evolution*. New York: Columbia University.

Posey, T. and Losch, M. 1983. "Auditory Hallucinations of Hearing Voices in 375 Normal Subjects." *Imagination, Cognition and Personality* 3:99–113.

Richards, I. 1936. *Philosophy of Rhetoric*. New York: Oxford University Press.

Swenson, L. 1972. *The Ethereal Aether: A History of the Michelson-Morley-Miller Aether-Drift Experiments, 1890–1930*. Austin: University of Texas Press.

Modelling of Mind/Brain Relationships

Antonio R. Damasio

The role of a neuroscientist in a conference on the mind is to appear in late eighteenth-century attire, disguised as a latter-day Franz Joseph Gall, and scandalize the audience by proclaiming that mind faculties can be related to bumps, not in the brain, but in the skull, in the best phrenological tradition. Although Gall has once again become an interesting thinker, I am afraid I will not succumb to the temptation. Instead I will proceed to state a few firm beliefs I have in this area:

Brain activity is responsible for the generation of the mental phenomena which we collectively designate as the mind.

The relations between brain and mind can, to a large extent, be elucidated by scientific inquiry.

Exploration of the concept of mind is possible not only from the standpoints of philosophy and psychology, but also from the perspective of neuroscience.

It is possible to build a bridge between neuroscience and cognitive science, even if the investigators in each of these broad fields utilize remarkably different methodological instruments and concentrate on phenomena of manifestly different natures, and the results of philosophical inquiry can have a bearing on either of the sciences and on their match. A corollary of this is that approaches from isolated methodologies are doomed.

I will outline a series of biological characteristics of neural units that indicate the role those units are likely to play in the generation of mind phenomena. Such characteristics are potentially useful for investigators engaged in delineating computational devices capable of performing "mind" acts.

I will discuss modelling constraints that pertain to the neuroanatomical and neurophysiological domains, at the level of cerebral cell assemblies that integrate neural networks. This essay will not entertain the domains of molecular and cellular neurobiology, which have a direct bearing on the cell-assembly level. The findings that constitute the basis for these constraints come from studies in which experimental cognitive and neuropsychological measurements were correlated with neuroanatomical data obtained in normal individuals, neurological patients with focal cerebral lesions, and in nonhuman primates. In several instances they are also based on electrophysiological data.

The following is a list of the constraints I will allude to:

Sensory information has rigid arrival points in the cerebral cortex.

First-order sensory information is restricted to the arrival-point cortex and to its vicinity.

Sensory processing "modules" for all sensory modalities are duplicated.

In spite of their duplication and their apparent gross anatomical symmetry, sensory-processing modules may have diverse intramodal specialization.

The extraction of features within a sensory modality occurs in parallel, not in series.

Memories of sensory experiences of a given modality are stored only in the processing module of the respective modality.

The geographical isolation of sensory-processing modules is obviated by the existence of integrative neural devices.

The brain is endowed with innate systems that are concerned with the maintenance of the organism's integrity and with the continuation of the species. Preprogrammed neural devices maintain the balance of the internal milieu by means of direct action on a variety of crucial organs and biological integrative systems, as well as by indirectly generating brain states that impel individuals, in more or less conscious form, to a variety of actions that culminate in food gathering, sexual activity, or flight from imminent danger.

Let us now consider some of these constraints.

Arrival and processing of information in the cerebral cortex. Figure 1 depicts a real human brain in which the classical areas of the cerebral

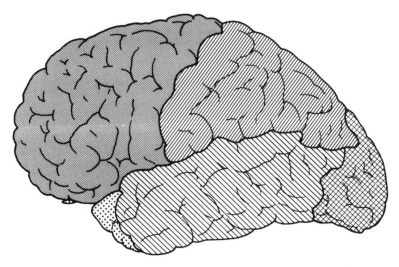

Figure 1. Above—drawing of the left side of the human brain (cerebrum) as seen from the outside; below—view of the left cerebral hemisphere from the inside (as seen on a cut through the center)

⊠ OCCIPITAL
▨ PARIETAL
⊡ LIMBIC
◩ TEMPORAL
◼ FRONTAL

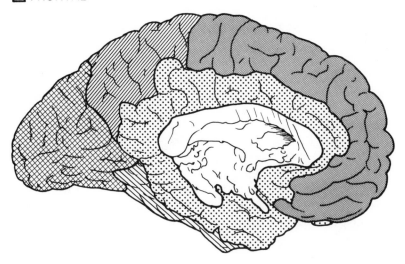

lobes have been depicted—the frontal, parietal, temporal, and occipital lobes, as well as an area called the limbic lobe, which surrounds the corpus callosum and which is visible mainly from the inside aspect of each hemisphere. These images tell us about something that has been a problem with much of the modelling of brain and mind relationships: the belief that we can proceed with valid brain/mind associations based on notions as gross as that of cerebral lobe, or left or right hemisphere. Although there is a large-scale relationship between these broad neuroanatomical units and higher brain function, the truth is that these so-called lobes really integrate a large number of anatomical units and, naturally, functional roles.

Another point that we should recall is that although any discussion of higher brain function always concentrates on the cerebral cortex—the outer shell of the brain—very many brain structures are not located in the outer shell, but are instead contained in deep gray nuclei such as the basal ganglia or the thalamus.

The vast expanse of the cerebral cortex is now seen to be composed of myriad units. The cortex is made up of billions of neurons distributed along its mantle, not in a haphazard manner but in a highly organized arrangement, with both horizontal and vertical patterns. When we look at the cortex in a section made perpendicular to its surface, we see that it has horizontal layers and that those layers are architectonically different. The neurons that constitute each of these layers are different in type, number, and spatial arrangement. They are not wired in a simple network in which everything connects with everything else; rather, they are wired with a rhyme and reason. In most instances, when you look at the first layer, the so-called superficial layer, you see that it is actually acellular and made up of connections between cells. In layer II and part of layer III you generally find cells that are linked to local circuitry and that process output to other areas of the brain, for instance to areas in the opposite hemisphere. In layers V or VI you find the origin of most of the cortical output systems. For instance, the large cells that compose the origin of the pyramidal tract originate in layer V.

The cerebral cortex also has other interesting characteristics. First, there is a vertical organization, so that you can imagine the cortex as a series of more or less cylindrical columns that are set next to each other, perpendicular to the cortical surface, as if the cortex were a long beehive. Each of these columnar units contains over one hundred neurons (the exception is in the visual cortex, where columns contain about 260 neurons each), vertically interconnected within the unit, and that is why the neurophysiological properties of a given cell column share many features. (The cell column is, in many respects, the central computational unit of the cerebral cortex. The communication between cell columns is carried out primarily by vertical input and output projection fibers, rather than by transverse, side-by-side crosstalk.) Second, when you look at the cortical mantle throughout the brain, you discover yet one more way in which it is *not* homogenous. If we were to flatten out the cortex and get rid of all its crevices and fissures, we would come up with a sheath of about 1000 square centimeters in surface area (incidentally, about ten times the area of the cortex in a rhesus monkey). Then, studying the cortex from area to area, we would discover that the architectural arrangement of the cortical columns was remarkably different, and that relatively small areas of cortex were as distinctive as different buildings in a street. A look at a section of brain in the visual cortex, for instance, would show precipitous changes as we moved from area 17 (the primary visual cortex, which most neuroanatomists would immediately recognize in the same way that they recognize the face of a friend) to nearby area 18. This is because layer IV of area 17 has characteristic dark bands which actually subdivide into four subsets. Nothing in the brain surface would lead you to predict that the cellular architecture of nearby area 18 is entirely different from that of area 17, no less so than the architecture of Mies Van Der Rohe's Seagram building is readily distinguishable from that of the buildings set beside it on Park Avenue. Naturally, the function of these different areas is quite different, something that both physiologic and cognitive experiments prove.

A section perpendicular to the motor cortex provides a comparable example. We can immediately recognize it as motor cortex because of pyramidal neurons seen in layer V. When you look at two adjoining regions of the frontal cortex, the frontal granular cortex of area 46 and the premotor cortex of area 6, you realize that the architecture is quite different. Is it not likely that the function these regions have to perform, as isolated modules, should also be different?

The brain has more than one hundred such areas of different architecture in each hemisphere—that is, at least one hundred different units capable of making different contributions to overall brain function (see Figure 2). In addition, there are subsets of these areas, we could call them ensembles of cell columns, that have functional subspecialization. These areas can be defined by neurophysiologic, neuroanatomic and neuropsychologic characteristics. The manner in which these different regions are linked to each other is anything but

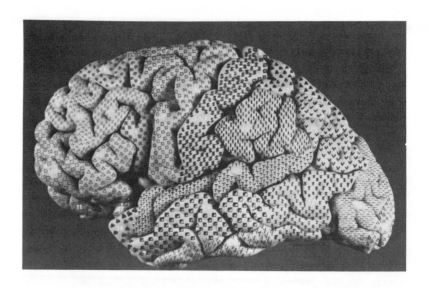

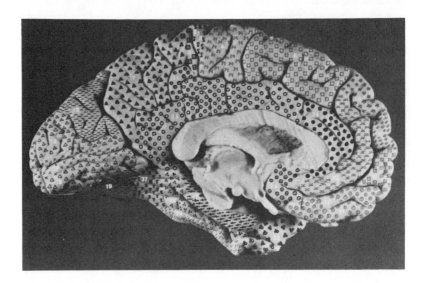

Figure 2. Photograph of a left human cerebrum corresponding to Figure 1, with different functional areas numbered and stippled in varying patterns

casual. Connections are highly patterned, and the notion that every area in the brain connects with every other area is simply a gross mistake. Any modelling of brain function predicated on that erroneous assumption is quite inappropriate. We know that the way structures interconnect is highly selective, any one of these numerous neural units not actually connecting with more than a dozen others. Communication between distant brain areas generally involves way stations, and there are few examples of structures that connect over remote distances or that connect in a blanket fashion over an entire hemisphere. True, there are some exceptions to this rule. Certain "servo-systems" of the brain, for instance, systems that provide the cerebrum with neurochemical mediators such as acetylcholine, norepinephrine, or dopamine, are somewhat promiscuous in their distribution across the cortex. But this is certainly not the case with the units of the cortex related to higher information processing.

Sensory information has rigid arrival points in the cerebral cortex. We can give an idea of this constraint by making an illustrative statement: you cannot possibly receive visual information in the auditory cortex, or vice versa. What does this mean? The information you are hearing at this very moment has to arrive in the auditory cortices only, and none of it will arrive in the visual or olfactory cortices, for instance. It is possible to bring a digest of that auditory information, at a secondary level of processing, in contact with visual or somatosensory information that you are also receiving at this moment. But, fortunately or unfortunately, that cannot be done within the same neural unit, because the brain machine is not designed that way. Computational models of perception have to take into account this particular feature.

Let us discuss briefly how information is routed to the central nervous system and use the visual system as an example. Visual information is processed along a complex chain of stations, from the retina, to the lateral geniculate nucleus, to the visual cortex of area 17. If you were to sever this system anywhere along the chain, depending on where you cut, you would produce remarkable but always different distortions of visual input. There are two major reasons why that is so. One is that each level of the hierarchical chain of visual units contributes a different product to the overall process. Another is that from the retina to the brain, the neurons carry a visual representation that maintains relationships among its components, a representation that closely simulates the relationships of the external stimuli that are optically projected into the retina. (I am of course taking the clear stand that I believe in the existence of an external reality that our nervous systems do their best to represent.) And so, it is not equivalent to stimulate a point in the periphery of your retina or in its center. When you receive visual information from the periphery of your visual field, in the periphery of your retina, that information arrives in a specific portion of the visual cortex that is dedicated to peripheral visual field information. This portion is located in the most anterior or rostral region of the visual calcarine cortex. When you receive information closer to the center of the visual field, it will be projected in a patterned, hardwired way into the more posterior or caudal region of the visual cortex. Only developmental disease, in utero or infancy, is able to tinker with such wiring patterns. In fact, all of the central information of the visual field, within the first ten degrees or so from its center, is going to be projected squarely into the most posterior end of the calcarine fissure. Furthermore, the information that comes from the top or from the bottom of the visual field, the superior or the inferior visual field, is not going to end in the brain in a casual way either. The information from the top will end up exclusively in the inferior aspect of the calcarine fissure, that is, the inferior component of the primary visual cortex or area 17. The information from the bottom of the visual field will go to the superior aspect of the calcarine fissure. Furthermore, the information that comes from the right visual field will go exclusively to the left visual cortices, and the information from the left will go to the right. This is a good example, at the level of perceptual systems, of how the brain is wired to bring in information. This wiring obeys fundamentally rigid patterns unless it suffers the influence of disease (erroneous genetic control of growth and contact of cells, infection, ischemia, etc.). But this should not be construed as meaning that neuron networks are unchangeable once they mature. Although our understanding of such processes is still preliminary, there is evidence that the patterns of neural communication can change with learning in a variety of subtle ways, e.g., change in the firing code of a neuron, changes in neurochemical mediators used for some input or output contacts, possible atrophy or strengthening of some synaptic contacts, etc.

The extraction of features within a sensory modality occurs in parallel, not in series. Another important modelling constraint comes from the fact that after information arrives in primary cortices and begins to be processed, the analysis of its component features appears to occur in parallel predominantly rather than in series. It used to be thought that information, for instance visual information, would arrive in the cortex and would be processed in a sequential form. Somehow form, movement, depth, color would all be extracted out of this same arrival point in a cascade of serially integrated units. There is no evidence that such is the case, and quite a lot of evidence to the contrary, i.e., the properties of visual information are first teased apart and only at a later stage in the processing are they serially integrated.

Consider the following examples. Figure 3 shows templates corresponding to a CT scan of a patient with a lesion in the right occipital

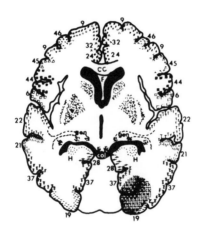

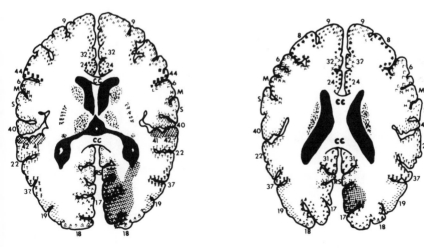

Figure 3. CT scan templates of a patient with a lesion (stippled) in the right occipital lobe, as seen from above, involving the calcarine region

lobe encompassing both the primary visual cortex and the association cortex above and below the calcarine region. The patient developed a *complete loss of all features of vision* in the field opposite the lesion; that is, for practical purposes the patient became blind for all features of vision in the left visual field, but function in the right visual field remained intact.

Figure 4 shows an apparently similar lesion that turns out to be remarkably different. The lesion is restricted to the lower portion of the right visual-association cortex. It never involves the area of the calcarine region where, in the primary visual cortex, the bulk of visual information arrives. Instead, damage encompasses a particular area of the brain which we know now is especially concerned with color processing at cortical level. And so what this patient experiences is a loss of *color vision* to the left of the vertical meridian, so that his field of vision has lost color in the left but not on the right. On the left side, where color is gone, form vision and vision of depth are still maintained, as is the vision of movement. This is a strong indication that the extraction of color is not performed in sequence, and can be disturbed without any other features of vision suffering a similar impairment. Other dissociations—for instance, the loss of stereoptic perception or of movement detection, without impairment of color vision—are also well known now.

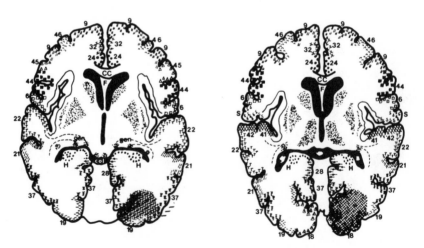

Figure 4. Similar to Figure 3, but the lesion in the right occipital lobe is limited to the lower part of the visual association cortex and spares the calcarine region

Areas in the superior occipital and parietal lobes in both man and monkey appear to have no interest in color but are interested, instead, in detection of movement and in the appreciation of depth. In general, they are devoted to the ability to perceive surrounding space in its multiple dimensions and to relate the body to that space. Patients with lesions in the occipito-parietal areas see color and form without any problem but have trouble with the appreciation of depth and the detection of movement.

Sensory-processing modules for all sensory modalities are duplicated. Another constraint that is of special interest in brain modelling has to do with the duplication of sensory-processing modules, in all sensory modalities. We appear to have two mirror-image brains—one on the left, another on the right. But duplication is more apparent than real. In many instances, each side (half) of the system is devoted to brain work related to the opposite side (half) of the body (this happens, for instance, in the primary sensory and motor systems). But on each side, the association cortices that surround the primary sensory arrival points are *not* functionally symmetric. They have specialized abilities and perform different tasks. Nor are they anatomically the true mirror images of each other, although a cursory look at their surface may leave that impression. For instance, we know that in the auditory cortex of about 70% of the population, the cytoarchitectonic area that lies just behind the primary auditory cortex, the planum temporale, is much larger on the left than on the right. This area happens to be, unequivocally, one of the most important structural components of the brain's language-processing apparatus.

When one of those visual areas discussed above is damaged on the left side, provided that damage falls in the appropriate region, patients develop a reading disorder. Damage in the mirror structure of the right side would not cause a reading disorder except in a minority of individuals with so-called crossed or mixed language dominance. Thus a corollary constraint can be formulated stating that, in spite of their duplication and their apparent gross anatomical symmetry, sensory-processing modules may have diverse intramodal specialization.

Memories of sensory experiences of a given modality are stored only in the processing module of the respective modality. There is evidence that the separate memories of visual or auditory experiences have to be laid down in the cortex of the appropriate denomination—for instance, visual or auditory—and in no other cortex. (Notwithstanding the fact that concurrent activation of separate memory traces from different memory systems is experienced as a polymodal, "sensory integrated" event.) The study of modality-specific disorders of recognition (the agnosias) supports this claim. Within each modality, separate cortices appear to be differently devoted to diverse classes of stimuli in the universe. An example can be found in a distinction that the visual cortex clearly honors, between the recognition of faces and other related stimuli, and the recognition of objects. Psychophysiological probes have recently helped confirm the existence of these intramodal memory traces.

The geographical isolation of sensory-processing modules is obviated by the existence of integrative neural devices. This is an important constraint. If the sensory information you are receiving now arrives in different cerebral cortices and is processed in the vicinity of the arrival point, how are you going to be able to create the necessarily composite memory of this lecture and be able later to recall a part of that memory, with both auditory and visual components, both verbal and nonverbal, and remember some of the concepts I have discussed? Clearly, in order to be able to achieve that, we must have systems in our brains that bring together information beyond the sensory-processing modules, beyond the primary and association cortices. Systems capable of doing that have now been described in animals and in man, and I will give one example: the system that brings information from all sensory cortices into the limbic system, by means of anatomical structures located in the medial temporal lobe. The region of the entorhinal cortex, the gateway to the hippocampus, is only one or two synapses away from the association cortices of all sensory modalities and from everything that is happening in them. Thus, the hippocampal cortices are rapidly privy to practically all the information that is being processed in those other cortices, and can probably compute the relationship between those different types of information that it integrates. Now, is the information arriving there in the same form of representation? Most likely it is not, not any more than when I experience seeing a red chair, I believe there is actually a red chair in my visual cortex. What I think there is, is a brain representation, a series of deformations and modifications in cellular structure, in cellular connectivity and neurochemical parameters, that permits the "symbolic" notation of that chair to exist in my visual cortex according to the computation of key physical elements in the chair, guided by a set of cognitive principles by now immanent in my brain. In all likelihood the hippocampus receives a physiological index of that previous notation. The hippocampus and its related cortices probably build secondary representations of a given stimulus and also build secondary representations of other stimuli that held temporal or spatial relationships with the given stimulus. We believe those integrated secondary representations are stored in yet other cortices, in lateral temporal lobe and in frontal lobe.

Integrative systems of this sort (and there are others in the brain) are absolutely fundamental if we are to build memories beyond the generic level. What is called *semantic* memory in Tulving's theory and which I call *generic* is a cognitive structure that requires only primary and association cortices for its mature operation. In order to build the highly specific *episodic* memories of Tulving which I call *contextual* memories, we need to bring together and integrate unique information from different modalities. If those contextual memories are related to us personally, we also need to integrate elements of time and correlations with our past history and future plans; we need to place those unique experiences in personal perspective. In all probability, such a computation can be achieved with the engineering devices available in anterior temporal lobe structures. If you tinker with those engineering devices as nature does, for instance, in patients with herpes simplex encephalitis in whom both temporal lobes are selectively and entirely demolished, the ability to create or recall contextual/personal memories is entirely destroyed. And yet, the preservation of single modality cortices—for instance, in the auditory and visual system—permits such patients to access generic memories and recall or recognize almost anything in the universe, provided they are not asked to bring any particular item into their own historical perspective. A similar condition also develops gradually in Alzheimer's disease and is one of the hallmarks of the multifaceted memory loss of that condition.

The brain is endowed with innate systems that are concerned with the maintenance of the organism's integrity and continuation of the species. This last constraint is of considerable importance because I happen to believe there are preprogrammed neural devices that maintain the internal milieu by means of action on a variety of crucial organs and biological integrative systems, as well as by indirectly generating brain states that impel individuals in more or less conscious form to a variety of actions that normally culminate in sexual activity, gathering of food, and so on. I also happen to believe that there are preprogrammed and hard-wired blueprints for many thought processes and that they are quite related to these basic-maintenance neural devices and to the continued transactions that human beings have had for a few million years with the external universe.

Concluding Remarks

I do not think that at birth the human mind and brain are a tabula rasa, as the British empiricists might have wanted us to believe. We are born with a considerable amount of *intellect* and *sense data*. Considering the evidence currently available in neuroscience and cognitive science, I believe that the relation between phenomena of brain activity and mind can be explored to the level of specified subcomponents of either. To the implicit assumption that the brain is the organ of the mind, we can add that phenomena of the mind are not to be seen as the products, in equipotential fashion, of *any* brain component. Rather, different brain components appear to be able to perform different physiological tasks and thus contribute, by means of organized neural-system networks, to the generation of certain phenomena of the mind.

There is no reason to believe that any of the phenomena of the mind will not come to be related to the activity of specific brain regions. I believe this is true even for such complex mental characterizations as the will. This position is antidualist, in the sense that it denies a separation and parallel operation for mind and brain. Nonetheless, a Kantian duality of sorts remains. Although I believe that all the phenomena of the mind are the result of activity of neural networks in the brain, I do not think that *mind* and *brain* are synonymous. The phenomena of the mind are the result of the coordinated activation of groups of neurons and of the coordinated interaction between their activities; that is, the activities and their interactions *become* mental phenomena, for a fragment of time; the neurons that permitted them may go back to a resting state. Curiously, this view is compatible with both Aristotle's and Aquinas's. Without a doubt, then, the phenomena of the mind are of a different nature than the anatomical structure or the neurophysiological responses that we study as neuroscientists, although they are closely interrelated.

But the fact that mind phenomena and neural phenomena are of necessarily different nature does not deny at all the physicality of the mind. The phenomena of the mind are as physical as is the activity within a microchip, or the transmission of radio waves, or the movement of physical particles we have never seen.

The problem of the "ghost in the machine," the ghost that Gilbert Ryle wanted to exorcise, is caused by our ignorance of both neuroscience and cognitive science and is prompted by our limited ability to describe processes that are not mechanical or electronic. In a way, the problem is that of finding adequate, powerful metaphors. The brain, or a complex system of computers, execute the "mind" function with complex processes which occur instantaneously and which we are at a loss to describe well, outside of some mathematical characterization. We can describe them as a logical system, but that is not describing the process itself. In essence, our problem is the discovery and narration of the physics of the mind. But the concept of the mind's physicality, and of its "brain-aboutness," poses, in my view, no problem whatsoever.

Suggested Readings

Afifi, A. and Bergman, R. 1985. *Basic Neuroscience*. Baltimore: Urban and Schwarzenberg.

Damasio, A. 1983. "Pure Alexia." *Trends in Neurosciences* 6:93–96.

———. 1985. "Prosopagnosia." *Trends in Neurosciences* 8:132–135.

Damasio, A. and Geschwind, N. 1984. "The Neural Basis of Language." *Annual Review of Neuroscience* 7:127–147.

Damasio, A., Yamada, T., Damasio, H., Corbett, J., and McKee, J. 1980. "Central Achromatopsia: Behavioral, Anatomic and Physiologic Aspects." *Neurology* 30:1064–1071.

Hyman, B., Van Hoesen, G., Damasio, A., and Barnes, C. 1984. "Alzheimer's Disease: Cell-Specific Pathology Isolates the Hippocampal Formation." *Science* 225:1168–1170.

Tranel, D. and Damasio, A. 1985. "Knowledge without Awareness: An Autonomic Index of Facial Recognition by Prosopagnosics." *Science* 228:1453–1454.

The Languages of Pain

David B. Morris

> He has seen but half the universe
> who has not been shown the house
> of pain—Ralph Waldo Emerson

Pain holds a prominent place in the history of tangled relations between body and mind. Its prominence derives at least in part from its mystery. Like other imperfectly understood and vaguely defined concepts, pain lends itself to opposing views. Consider, for example, the opposition between two major systems or models for explaining pain: medicine and theology. Western medicine (in its various historical forms) has regularly explained pain as a symptom which permits us to infer facts about the state of the body. Pain, in this simplified biomedical model, is regarded mainly as a problem of tissue damage. Mind—whether belonging to the physician or to the patient—functions somewhat like a detached observer, registering or reporting what pain tells us about the body. Everyday experience sometimes seems to confirm such an extreme separation. An impacted wisdom tooth or an inflamed appendix possesses an uncanny power of suspending thought. Such pain, if only for brief periods, can reduce us to creatures who seem all body.

In contrast to the body-centered traditions of Western medicine with their emphasis on tissue damage, Western theology has tended to regard pain as closely related to our spiritual states. Bodies—like printed words on the page—achieve a kind of transparency as we look through or beyond them. Saint Sebastian in Renaissance paintings never seems to notice all those arrows protruding from his torso. His eyes are usually raised above the plane of bodies. Pain, in this simplified theological model, leads to an order of experience which ultimately breaks contact with the animal biochemistry of nerves and neurotransmitters. The ills of the body—from Job's boils to Captain Ahab's stump—possess a metaphysical rather than a physical significance. They suggest how far a creature of mind or spirit may challenge the common heritage of flesh, bone, and earth.

My purpose in sketching this simplified contrast between medicine and theology is to locate two extreme positions which reflect the familiar dualism in our attitudes toward pain. If our pain grows severe enough, first we call the doctor. Then—should medicine fail us—we will consider consulting the priest. Of course, this extreme dualism does not fairly represent the outlook of specific churches or clinics or persons in pain, where divisions are less extreme, less doctrinaire. Indeed, by introducing the dualism of a pain which is all body or all mind I wish to focus on the complex situations in which an understanding of pain must renounce the sharp edges of simplified contrast. Pain, I want to argue, is a phenomenon which forces us to explore the complicated interdependence of body and mind. In exploring this interdependence, I want to ask a quite specific question which falls outside the traditional concerns of medicine and theology. What happens to pain when it enters the zone of language? Or—put a little differently—how does language affect the relations among mind, body, and pain?

The most fundamental relation between language and pain is one of betrayal. The term *betrayal* is appropriate here because it includes two distinct and almost contrary senses—to reveal and to misrepresent—and these two senses of betrayal are inextricably entangled in the experience of pain. In the sense of revealing pain, language exposes something which otherwise might remain entirely concealed. Like the noises children sometimes make playing hide and seek, our speech acts give pain a means of becoming semivisible, emerging from utter privacy into a dialogical context. These revelations need not be complex or premeditated. As John H. Dirckx, M.D., writes, "The genuine animal cry of pain, like vocal signs of surprise, fear, anger, or joy, results from a sudden expulsion of breath, which is part of a general bodily response." This elemental language of the body—uttered perhaps without anyone within earshot and without implicit claims to dialogue—belongs to a continuum which includes vastly intricate spoken and unspoken communications. Indeed, the statement "I am in pain" is seldom a simple revelation of fact or feeling, but invokes complex and implicit social relations which bind the speaker and listener, which define a range of appropriate and of inappropriate responses.

The revelation of a private, personal, internal state is often compounded with a stronger sense of betrayal. Language also betrays pain when it misrepresents something which cannot easily or perhaps entirely be put into words. Although we commonly imagine pain as full of noise and shouts, there is a muteness which is equally typical. Patients quickly learn to suppress complaints which grow tedious to family and staff, even as staff and family learn to ignore complaining patients. But these bedside games simply intensify a silence which already exists at the heart of pain. No one has better expressed the inexpressibility of pain than Emily Dickinson in the following knotty two-stanza poem:

> Pain—has an Element of Blank—
> It cannot recollect
> When it begun—or if there were
> A time when it was not
>
> It has no Future—but itself—
> Its Infinite contain
> Its Past—enlightened to perceive
> New Periods—of Pain.

The blankness which Dickinson describes tends to defeat language: to collapse conscious distinctions between past and future into an endless, undifferentiated present, reshaping our familiar multicolored landscapes into a bleak, grey uniformity. There is very little that language can tell us of such a state without falsifying it, without imposing upon it words which simply do not apply, which belong to an altogether alien order of experience.

In the language of pain, a continuous mingling of revelation and of misrepresentation points to an underlying paradox. What our words often reveal is the impossibility of finding words adequate to our experience. This paradox is not a mere semantic or logical puzzle. It accurately reflects the problems of an interdependent relation between mind and body. There is no outside post available for a fully detached and fully adequate description of pain. Language, we might say, makes the body present to the mind—allows us to think and to rethink our experience—but this presence almost inevitably exhausts the powers of language, yielding to a stammering, tongue-tied speech or to frustrated silence. In response to this troublesome wordlessness of pain, clinicians sometimes employ a version of the McGill Pain Assessment Questionnaire, in which patients are asked to choose among an extensive series of carefully grouped adjectives. Is your pain flashing, jumping, searing, tearing, sour, throbbing, dull? There are good reasons why specific adjectives are grouped together, reflecting (for example) measurable differences in the transmission of pain impulses through different nerve fibres. As a diagnostic instrument, the McGill questionnaire has valuable, if strictly limited, uses. In another sense, however, it organizes and emphasizes the betrayal of pain by language. A grid of preselected adjectives proves little more than a coarse net for catching a species of invisible or semiinvisible prey.

Language not only betrays pain, as I have argued. My second major claim is that it also historicizes pain. Indeed, the historicity of pain is equally fundamental in shaping and defining what we feel, and here too an attention to language helps to expose the complex interdependence of body and mind. Language, I want to argue in what follows, contributes to the historicity of pain in three main areas. It draws pain into time, into culture, and into the process of interpretation. Interpretation, culture, and time, in turn, reinforce the interdependence of body and mind so basic to pain. Let us therefore consider what happens to pain as language draws it relentlessly into history.

The crucial role of time in the experience of pain is seldom acknowledged, because we habitually—and rightly—refer to suffering as somehow an eternal or timeless state. In this synchronic dimension, pain is an experience which unites us across centuries with distant civilizations and with nameless ancestors, even as it tends to blot out past and future. This authentic timelessness, however, must not blind us to an important diachronic, historical dimension of pain, visible across eras and borders. As in the changes which differentiate the English word *ouch* from similar interjections in French, in German, and in classical Greek, even an event so spontaneous and apparently so timeless as a cry of pain does not occur—after infancy—outside a historical, linguistic context which shapes and limits our range of expression. This shaping force of time will be more evident when we consider, momentarily, how language draws pain into culture.

Time, however, has another major influence upon the experience of pain, which more clearly exposes the interdependence of body and mind. Modern medicine, in its distinction between acute pain and chronic pain, reminds us that time imparts a qualitative difference to acts of suffering. Acute pain is familiar to everyone who has stubbed a toe or broken a bone. We endure such pain recognizing that its causes are well known, its duration limited, its outcome predictable. Chronic pain—commonly defined as pain which lasts more than six months—is quite different. Its causes are often not well understood—or remain mysterious. Treatment, even when organic causes are clear, seems unable to provide lasting relief. As distinguished from acute pain, chronic pain cannot be considered simply a reflex of the body. It is as if the body's alarm system has malfunctioned and no one can turn off the alarm. Time thus creates a situation in which the mind begins to brood upon experience in ways which often alter the experience itself. Fear, remorse, self-pity, muscular resistance, depression: these common responses to pain can combine with what clinicians call "secondary gain"—a perception that our suffering may bring with it desirable side-effects. A formerly inattentive spouse grows suddenly tender and caring. Disability payments prove a welcome substitute for hard labor or insecure employment. Pain now begets new pain in a classic feedback loop.

Culture contributes as much as temporality to shaping the experience of pain. The mind which broods upon injury or suffering broods within a specific community. It required modern insurance companies and welfare systems to transform pain into a commodity, and even our habit of referring pain automatically to a medical context reflects specific—if now widely shared—cultural predispositions. What I wish to claim is that the language of a community and the values implicit in particular forms of expression help to shape our experience of pain. To come down with "the miseries" or "the blues" is to place our experience within categories which certain cultures or subcultures make available—and others ignore. It is now permissible for Fortune 500 executives to suffer from something called stress. Indeed, companies across America now offer top employees practical minicourses in stress management. On the city streets, on the farm, on the beach, language provides far different categories for making sense of what we feel. Such language not only describes behavior and feeling but, quite clearly, influences them as well. In English the word *pain* normally refers to physical discomfort. In France, the cognate form (*peine*) implies mental distress or somewhat abstract "troubles."

The influence of cultural systems upon the experience of pain is even more evident within theology than within the languages of medicine. Thus, Christianity has often regarded pain as a process of purification; Islam tends to regard pain as a trial which exercises the supreme virtue of patience; in Judaism, by contrast, pain is regarded as an unmitigated evil, a curse. Anthropologists and psychologists have published numerous studies describing the idiosyncratic systems which specific cultures or subcultures devise for handling pain. Jews and Italians respond to pain with a flood of language, while Eskimos—who possess those famous thirteen different words for snow—seem to deal with pain by ignoring it. Closer to home, it is obvious that to American males raised on John Wayne films, pain was closely associated with a cultural standard of manliness which emphasized strength and silence. By contrast, this cultural relation between pain and gender is neatly reversed by the Third World tribe in which women resume working several hours after giving birth in the fields, while the husband retreats to his bed and spends the next few days groaning loudly. Language alone, of course, cannot sustain or create such rituals. But our words and concepts come to us already saturated with cultural values, and even in opposing the values of our culture we are forced to acknowledge them—to adopt and to perpetuate the very terms we reject in order to reject them.

In its historicity, pain not only teaches us the specific forms and values which it assumes within specific periods and distinct cultures. It also initiates a more active, visible process of participation in the ills of the body which I will call, generally, interpretation. Interpretation is a process of making or of finding meaning, and meaning is fundamentally—although not exclusively—an activity of language. Like recent philosophers, anthropologists, and literary theorists, I want to consider the act of interpretation as profoundly linguistic, as inseparable from the explicit or implicit dialogues through which we arrive at knowledge. Pain cannot be considered purely timeless or private because one of the most important things we do with pain—primarily by means of language—is to make sense of it, to interpret it, to seek to know it.

The importance of interpretation in considering pain is something I can convey most economically by sketching an argument which I am developing elsewhere at the length required to make it persuasive. Here I will hope for mere clarity rather than persuasiveness. Pain, I want to argue, despite its clear and persistent reference to the body, has a long history as something which engages us in an effort to ascribe or to attribute meaning. Indeed, in earlier periods and in other cultures pain has been understood *primarily* as an occasion which demands an encounter with meaning. Meaning (and the value which often accompanies meaning) must somehow be ascribed or attributed to pain in order to make pain comprehensible, to bring it within the boundaries of what is tolerable. Pain, in some accounts, even possesses or calls forth a visionary power which transforms the world which contains it. We must avoid the erroneous assumption that the experience of pain and the encounter with meaning are separate activities, one belonging to the body, the other to the mind. Mind and body are equally invested in the process of ascribing a meaning to pain. How we interpret pain will often directly affect the pain we feel.

My most pressing interest in the languages of pain centers on the occasions when the body becomes a source or subject of interpretation. It is not the physiology or pharmacology of pain which concerns me so much as what might be called the hermeneutics of pain. Yet, this distinction must not be pressed too hard. Physiology and pharmacology are themselves structures for interpreting pain, for making sense of what we feel, and—like other historical, cultural systems of explanation—they have generated their distinctive languages, saturated with the values which attend modern scientific activity. My inquiry thus cannot ignore the important process of interpretation which is inseparable from the ongoing research in numerous laboratories and clinics where pain slowly unfolds its secrets. The interpretation of pain, however, extends far beyond the borders of biomedical research, and I am concerned with the various far-flung historical systems which mankind has devised for making sense of pain. Most of these systems, in fact, belong to the areas studied traditionally in the humanities or human sciences. We find them a recurring presence in literature, in philosophy, in theology, in anthropology, in art, and in history, where the record of mankind's encounter with pain constitutes a variorum of differing interpretations.

The interpretations of pain from Homer to Samuel Beckett is obviously a subject I cannot explore here. Yet, a few illustrations may prove useful in suggesting how pain—as something we make sense of—has continued to change. For early man, the puzzle of pain had a clear solution. Pain was a punishment sent by the gods. Indeed, the concept of punishment is inscribed in the word *pain*, which derives from the Latin *poena* or "punishment." While Aristotle provided an influential account of pain as a biological concept, he also recognized that pain, like pleasure, belongs to the domain of ethics. Indeed, many Greek tragedies develop the possibility that pain initiates us in the clarifications and discoveries which we rightly call learning. Even where the treatment of pain seems deliberately stylized according to established literary conventions, we must ask what such conventions tell us. In *The Iliad*, for example, Greeks and Trojans suffer terrifying injuries, described in graphic detail. Few warriors, however, no matter how frightful their wounds, are represented as suffering pain. (Occasionally Homer mentions pain as prelude to a scene of medical treatment in which the pain then disappears.) This general silence appears especially deliberate when both Aphrodite and Ares are wounded in Book 5. The shrieks and bellows of these immortal gods contrast dramatically with the mortal warriors who expire in a soundless black mist—or who retire quietly for medication. Homer offers us a world in which violence is overrepresented and pain is underrepresented. It is a vision directly contrary to the elegy, where violence recedes and pain discovers new powers of eloquence. Satire provides still another form for making sense of pain, as language itself—like the primitive curse— provides a weapon for tormenting one's enemies and (as Jonathan Swift put it) for vexing the reader.

Although medicine has always served as an important system for ascribing sense or meaning to pain, it is part of my argument that the modern history of pain brings us to a moment of profoundest change, when the interpretation of pain passes from the intersecting discourses of medicine and of the humanities into the sole possession of medicine. I do not mean to parody this process of gradual change (which is not yet complete) by suggesting a cataclysmic and absolute fissure. Nor do I mean to belittle the magnificent achievements in recent medical knowledge of pain. In transferring major responsibility for understanding pain to medicine alone, however, we have not recognized how much remains unknown. Confronted with the mysteries of chronic pain, medical knowledge cannot yet supply the unambiguous answers and effective relief which we seek. Estranged from its ancient alliance with the humanities, pain too has changed. We have entered a time when pain threatens to become—outside the private languages of medicine—entirely drained of meaning. Meaningless pain is not simply beyond speech, as if wrapped in a Dickinsonian blankness, inaccessible to words. It is experience about which there is nothing to say, unless meaninglessness itself becomes a subject for meditation. There is little relief, I suspect, in such meditations, and meaningless pain— deprived of language altogether—may rapidly and closely approach the inhuman.

Annotated Bibliography

The best technical but readable discussion of pain is by Ronald Melzack and Patrick D. Wall, *The Challenge of Pain* (New York: Basic Books, 1983). It contains an up-to-date bibliography of medical research. Continuing research is published or reviewed in two specialized journals. They are *Pain: The Journal of the International Association for the Study of Pain* and *Pain: Current Concepts on Pain and Analgesia*.

Several books written for general readers seek to place medical knowledge in a wider context, both social and historical. See, for example, Richard Serjeant, *The Spectrum of Pain* (London: Rupert Hart-Davis, 1969); Samuel Mines, *The Conquest of Pain* (New York: Grosset & Dunlap, 1974); Peter Fairley, *The Conquest of Pain* (1978; rpt. New York: Scribners, 1980); and H. B. Gibson, *Pain and its Conquest* (London: Peter Owen, 1982). Thereafter, two types of books generally divide the field. First, numerous self-help therapies, such as David E. Bressler's excellent *Free Yourself from Pain* (New York: Simon & Schuster, 1979). These are often written by doctors and are sometimes openly exploitative. Second, highly technical studies in medical subspecialties. Some representative technical studies include Richard Sternback, *Pain: A Psychophysiological Analysis* (London: Academic Press, 1968); Mark Mehta, *Intractable Pain* (London: W. B. Saunders, 1973); and *Diagnosis and Treatment of Chronic Pain*, ed. Nelson Hendler, Donlin M. Long, and Thomas N. Wise (London: John Wright, 1982). For work by two leaders in the field of pain research, see *Chronic Pain: Further Observations from City of Hope National Medical Center*, ed. Benjamin L. Crue, Jr., M.D. (New York: Spectrum, 1978) and various publications written or edited by John J. Bonica, M.D., beginning with his classic study *The Management of Pain* (Philadelphia: Lea and Febiger, 1953).

Some important texts emphasizing a medical perspective nonetheless seek to consider historical, psychological, political, and social aspects of medical knowledge. See, for example, K. D. Keele, *Anatomies of Pain* (Oxford: Blackwell Scientific Publications, 1957); Thomas S. Szasz, M.D., *Pain and Pleasure: A Study of Bodily Feelings* (New York: Basic Books, 1975); and Helen Neale, *The Politics of Pain* (New York: McGraw-Hill, 1978). W. Noordenbos includes an opening chapter on language in *Pain* (London: Elsevier, 1959). For an account by a physician active in the pain-clinic movement, see C. Norman Shealy, *The Pain Game* (Millbrae, Cal.: Celestial Arts, 1976).

The medical understanding of pain shades into studies in religion, theology, and theodicy. Useful book-length studies in this area include David Bakan, *Disease, Pain and Sacrifice: Toward a Psychology of Suffering* (Boston: Beacon, 1971); Steven F. Brena, *Pain and Religion: A Psychophysiological Study* (Springfield, Ill.: Thomas, 1968); G. A. Buttrick, *God, Pain and Evil* (Nashville, Tenn.: Abingdon, 1966); Kazoh Kitamori, *Theology of the Pain of God* (Richmond, Va.: John Knox Press, 1965); Louis Lavalle, *Evil and Suffering* (New York: Macmillan, 1963); C. S. Lewis, *The Problem of Pain* (1940; rpt. New

York: Macmillan, 1962); and Ferdinand Sauerbruch, *Pain: Its Meaning and Significance* (London: Allen & Unwin, 1963). A longer listing of such studies would include important work by John Bowker, John Ferguson, George Pitcher, and Roger Trigg.

Pain is a recurrent topic in the philosophy of mind, especially as influentially discussed by Gilbert Ryle and then debated by his followers and opponents. Other helpful philosophical texts include J. L. Cowan, *Pleasure and Pain: A Study in Philosophical Psychology* (London: Macmillan, 1968); Rem B. Edwards, *Pleasures and Pains: A Theory of Qualitative Hedonism* (Ithaca, N.Y.: Cornell University Press, 1979); and J. C. Wordsworth, *Pain and Other Problems: A Criticism of Modern Philosophies* (London: Allen & Unwin, 1954). The literature in journals is extensive. A few examples: Marcus B. Hester, "Wittgenstein's Analysis of I Know I Am In Pain," *Journal of Philosophy* 4 (1966): 274–279; G. Lewis, "The Place of Pain in Human Experience," *Journal of Medical Ethics* 4 (1978): 122–125; Daniel M. Taylor, "The Logical Privacy of Pains," *Mind* 79 (1970): 78–91. I am particularly impressed by the work of Roland Puccetti, which crosses the border between philosophy and neuroanatomy. See, for example, "Neural Plasticity and the Location of Mental Events," *Australian Journal of Philosophy* 52 (1974): 154–162; "The Great C-Fiber Myth: A Critical Note," *Philosophy of Science* 44 (1977): 303–305; "Pearce on Behalf of the Materialist," *Canadian Journal of Philosophy* 8 (1978): 157–162; and "The Ascent of Consciousness," in *Pragmatism and Purpose: Essays Presented to Thomas A. Goudge*, ed. L. W. Sumner et al. (Toronto: University of Toronto Press, 1981), pp. 199–206.

A welcome addition to historical writing on pain is Martin S. Pernick's *A Calculus of Suffering* (New York: Columbia University Press, 1984), which deals with attitudes toward pain and suffering in nineteenth-century America, drawing materials from both medicine and literature. Also highly relevant are Michel Foucault's *Discipline and Punish: The Birth of the Prison*, tr. Alan Sheridan (New York: Pantheon, 1977) and Michael Ignatieff's *A Just Measure of Pain: The Penitentiary in the Industrial Revolution, 1750–1850* (New York: Pantheon, 1978). Art history makes a contribution to the study of pain in Samuel Y. Edgerton's *Pictures and Punishment: Art and Criminal Prosecution during the Florentine Renaissance* (Ithaca, N.Y.: Cornell University Press, 1984). The political uses of pain are studied at a distance by Pieter Spierenburg, *The Spectacle of Suffering: Executions and the Evolution of Repression—from a Pre-industrial Metropolis to the European Experience* (Cambridge: Cambridge University Press, 1984)—and studied close up in the Amnesty International publication *Torture in the Eighties* (London: Amnesty International Publications, 1984). James Crewdson Turner has written on pain in relation to the treatment of animals, in *Reckoning with the Beast: Animals, Pain, and Humanity in the Victorian Mind* (Baltimore: Johns Hopkins University Press, 1980), while Daniel de Moulin offers "A Historical-Phenomenological Study of Bodily Pain in Western Man," *Bulletin of the History of Medicine* 48 (1974): 540–570.

There are no useful studies of pain in literature. The subject must be approached indirectly, through the many discussions of tragic catharsis in classical tragedy; through general studies of Romanticism, such as Mario Praz, *The Romantic Agony*, tr. Angus Davidson, 2nd ed. (London: Oxford University Press, 1951), or Althea Hayter, *Opium and the Romantic Imagination* (Berkeley: University of California Press, 1968); and through thematic studies, such as Reinhard Kuhn, *The Demon of Noontide: Ennui in Western Literature* (Princeton: Princeton University Press, 1976). Clearly, none of these studies approaches the subject of pain thoroughly or directly. The writer who brings us closest to pain as a theme or subject is, of course, de Sade. See, for example, the chapter entitled "De Sade and the Music of Cruelty" in Philip P. Hallie, *Cruelty* (1969; rpt. Middletown, Conn.: Wesleyan University Press, 1982). The journal *Tel Quel* devoted its entire Winter 1967 issue (vol. 28) to de Sade, on whom the scholarly literature is growing rapidly.

Largely ignored in treatments of pain are works or accounts written by people who have lived closely with pain. Three books I have found useful are Viktor E. Frankl, *From Death Camp to Existentialism: A Psychiatrist's Path to a New Therapy* (Boston: Beacon, 1959); Barbara Wolf, *Living with Pain* (New York: Seabury Press, 1977); and Mark Zborowski, *People in Pain* (San Francisco: Jossey-Bass, 1969).

I should emphasize that this selected bibliography is highly compressed. A full bibliography would include books important for my approach, even though they do not specifically deal with pain (such as Susan Sontag's brilliant study *Illness as Metaphor* [New York: Random House, 1973]). It would also cite numerous specialized essays, both on and slightly off my subject. (See, for example, Horacio Fabrega and Stephen Tyma, "Language and Cultural Influences in the Description of Pain," *British Journal of Medical Psychology* 49 [1976]: 349–371; and Sandra L. Bentman, "The Language of Grief," *Mosaic* 15 [1982]: 153–163. For a review of texts and work relevant to studies such as mine, see G. S. Rousseau, "Literature and Medicine: The State of the Field," *Isis* 72 (1981): 406–424.

Finally, although it appeared too late for use in this essay, I want to recommend highly the groundbreaking study of physical, linguistic, and political dimensions of pain, in topics ranging from war and torture to the Old Testament and the artistic text: Elaine Scarry's *The Body in Pain: The Making and Unmaking of the World* (New York: Oxford University Press, 1985). It undertakes the kind of multidisciplinary understanding which is absolutely essential to an adequate knowledge of pain and of its significance. It is a superb book.

Where Is Creativity?

D. N. Perkins

Where is creativity? Is it in the mind or in the brain? Does it lie in our goals, our attitudes, our thinking strategies? Does it come as part of the "original equipment" coded in our genes or as a spin-off of tolerant parents and nonrepressive surroundings? If all of these contribute in their distinctive ways, then with what mix and meld? Is creativity part of intelligence, something orthogonal to intelligence, or something oblique to intelligence? In short, how do we place creativity as a human trait in relation to the landscape of other traits like intelligence, causes like inheritance or learning, and constructs like mind versus brain?

Such questions are depressingly complex and daunting for a reason beyond complexity: they ask us to place creativity relative to some landmarks the positions of which we do not know with surety either, such as intelligence, the mind-body problem, and the nature-nurture issue. There are even risks of mistaking what encompasses what, much as a child, asked for the capital of Arkansas, may tell you that it is Utah.

As the history of mapmaking plainly shows, the geography may lie there waiting to be discovered, but maps of it do not emerge full-blown from the hand of the first cartographer. Initial maps are partial, sketchy, out of proportion, parochial in their compass. Later maps revise, correct, refine, and gradually converge toward the real. While maps render the actual geography of rivers and mountains, they also present and even participate complexly in human reality-making, where boundaries between states and nations are created by stipulation rather than nature. The same might hold with maps of mind, where the relations between, for instance, creativity and intelligence, may be more a matter of where boundaries are most comfortably and cogently placed than what the geography of brain or mind dictates. With such cartographer's caveats in mind, let us consider the terrain.

What Is Intelligence?

Here a broad perspective is essential. If one begins with a specialist's conception of intelligence, many questions quickly get begged. A generalist's conception makes a safer start: intelligence means intellectual competence. When we say that John or Jane is intelligent, or an intelligent manager, chess player, writer, or mathematician, we mean that John or Jane displays intellectual competence in general, or in the domain mentioned. Psychometric conceptions of intelligence move from that general notion of intellectual competence to a technical conception spurred by an important empirically observed phenomenon. People who display more or less intellectual competence for some tasks tend to do likewise for others. For some investigators, then, intelligence becomes whatever trait cuts across a diversity of tasks to account parsimoniously for good performance in many intellectual contexts.

But there is more than one way to construe intelligence as a cross-cutting intellectual competency, nor do all agree that the whole story on intellectual competency is told by intelligence. The contemporary psychology of intelligence encompasses some very diverse viewpoints. It's useful, in fact, to distinguish three broad perspectives on intelligence; they might be called *power models, tactical models,* and *knowledge* models of intellectual competence. A few words about each will reveal what the issues are.

Power theories of intelligence treat intellectual competence as one or several relatively basic computational powers. A person with more of a certain power processes a certain sort of information in certain ways faster and more accurately, with the consequence of better performance on complex intellectual tasks involving that kind of information. Power theories differ among themselves in two broad respects: what the powers are and whether they are subject to training.

The classic power theory is the univocal g for general intelligence.

Arthur Jensen, a contemporary advocate of a one-power theory, holds that g reflects the basal rate at which a person's nervous system can process information and handle complexity (Jensen 1984). He defends this position by a series of experimental studies in which he and others have shown correlations of the order of .4 between g as measured by complex intellectual tasks and certain parameters of a very simple reaction-time task. The reaction-time tasks come close to measuring raw intelligence, in Jensen's view, without any overlays from schooling or strategizing. Jensen avers that people do not improve on this task with practice and concludes that intelligence so understood is an intrinsic property of the nervous system not subject to learning, although, of course, one might learn to use better whatever intelligence one has. While Jensen's views can be criticized on a number of points (Longstreth 1984), it's hard to dismiss the accumulated evidence in its entirety.

A very different view of intelligence comes from Howard Gardner's recent theory of multiple intelligences (Gardner 1983). Gardner proposes no fewer than seven distinct intelligences with specialized functions: linguistic, spatial, musical, logical-mathematical, and three others. According to Gardner, each of us has each of these intelligences to varying degrees. Each intelligence corresponds to a subsystem of the nervous system specialized to deal with a certain kind of information: language and languagelike situations, spatial matters, and so on. Psychologists have missed these seven intelligences in part because tests of intelligence have ranged but narrowly, emphasizing linguistic and visual-spatial tasks. Training does not improve the basic information-processing power of an intelligence, but typically figures crucially in realizing its potential.

J. P. Guilford's theory of the structure of intelligence offers yet another variation on the power theme (Guilford 1967; Guilford and Hoepfner 1971). Based on factor-analytic studies, Guilford proposed 120 distinct components of intelligence, a number arrived at by taking in combination several different kinds of generic content such as numbers and notations versus words and ideas, several different mental operations such as remembering versus divergent thinking, and several different kinds of intellectual products such as classes versus implications. In Guilford's view, any of the 120 can be improved by training. Jensen and others argue, however, that Guilford's theory is an overcomplicated structure not at all justified by the precarious factor-analytic techniques employed (Jensen 1984; Horn and Knapp 1973; Sternberg 1977).

Tactical theories of intelligence locate intellectual competence in the strategies, metacognitive knowledge, and cognitive styles that a person can bring to bear on a task, rather than in the speed and efficiency of component operations. Better problem solvers, for instance, reach solutions more reliably because they pay heed to defining what the problem is, take the time to investigate several paths toward a solution, review their progress along the way, and check their answers.

Perhaps the most dramatic evidence for a tactical view of intelligence comes from work comparing retardates and normal individuals on memory and other tasks. Baron (1978) reviews a number of findings that show the same pattern. For instance, in unguided performance on simple memory tasks, retardates and young children score substantially below normal individuals. They also do not employ simple rehearsal strategies that older normal children exercise. When one guides the poor performers in employing such strategies, their achievements shoot up nearly to the level of the older normal children. This argues that the crucial factor is not raw memory power, as a power theory might hold, but the strategic application of the memory power available.

Mathematical problem solving is another area where good tactics have been shown to make a dramatic difference. Professional mathematicians solve problems by exercising, often without awareness, a number of heuristics first identified by Polya (1954, 1957) and later extended and elaborated by others (Wickelgren 1974; Schoenfeld 1980, 1982). In a recent teaching experiment, Alan Schoenfeld taught college students to become much better mathematical problem solvers during a one-month intensive course by guiding them in the persistent use of such straightforward heuristics as drawing a diagram to represent a problem, relating a problem to prior problems, solving a simpler related problem first, and monitoring one's progress so as to change directions if an approach did not yield progress (Schoenfeld 1982; Schoenfeld and Herrmann 1982).

Unlike power theories of intelligence, the tactical view of intelligence does not sort neatly into opposing theories advanced by particular individuals. Rather, various authors emphasize somewhat different lists of strategies, cognitive styles, and metacognitive knowledge, often directed at specific performances, and they usually do not contend that their lists are exhaustive or definitive.

Unlike power and tactical theories, knowledge theories do not accept the notion that intellectual competence is general across tasks. Rather, one needs a different theory of competency for each specialty.

Intellectual competence is highly context-bound, dependent on a deep, well-practiced knowledge of the ins and outs of a particular domain rather than on the raw power of a mental computer or on general strategies.

The classic findings here concern expertise in chess (Chase and Simon 1973; de Groot 1965). Chess makes a particularly apt example because on the surface it seems to be a game of logic, requiring the player to reason in general patterns that might well apply to other domains: "If I do this, my opponent will do that, but if I do this other thing, my opponent can't." The power of one's logic computer and good general reasoning tactics both might enable such thinking. However, investigations of chess mastery have yielded a rather different picture. Chess mastery depends on a very large mental repertoire of patterns of play specific to chess and irrelevant to other intellectual performances. The chess master does not out-compute or out-strategize the novice in any sense more general than chess; the chess master out-*knows* the novice. This knowledge does not take the form of articulated precepts but rather visual patterns evoked reflexively as the chess master examines a board and contemplates a line of play.

Chess is not the only area where such evidence has emerged. Studies of problem solving in physics, mathematics, and computer programming have revealed a similar role for a large repertoire of patterns or schemas specific to the performance in question (Chi, Feltovich, and Glaser 1981; Larkin, McDermott, Simon, and Simon 1980; Schoenfeld and Herrmann 1982; Soloway and Ehrlich 1982). Indeed, the work of Schoenfeld, cited earlier as an example of the tactical view, presents in some ways a borderline case. While many of Schoenfeld's strategies apply just as well to physics, chemistry, or everyday practical problem solving, others like "Use mathematical induction" are quite specific to mathematics. Furthermore, the effectiveness of Schoenfeld's strategies depends, of course, on the students having a significant knowledge base in mathematics to give them some substance for the strategies to manipulate.

In summary, at least three very different perspectives on intelligence exist today—power theories, tactical theories, and knowledge theories. Within each type, inevitably there is some disagreement as to which particular theory serves best. How to make provisional sense of the tangle for present purposes becomes the question, a question conveniently pursued by linking it to another one.

Intelligence in Mind and Brain

Where is intelligence—in the mind or in the brain? The question baldly put is too ambiguous to answer; one first needs to sort out various readings of it. A classic reading concerns the traditional mind-body problem. If we suppose that every mind event correlates one-to-one with some brain event, then clearly asking whether intelligence lies in mind or brain yields an inevitable and uninteresting *both*. Whatever intelligence-related event occurs in mind, its correlated event, equally concerned with intelligence, occurs in brain. Personally, I am willing to assume that there is such a correlation rule, although it is very hard to discover and, if discovered, probably too complex to be interesting.

However, two other readings of the question call for more careful examination. Sometimes when people contrast mind and brain they imagine something like the distinction between software and hardware. The hardware of the brain is the original equipment, perhaps improved by organic growth and development, while the software is the overlay of knowledge and knowhow that gives the brain something to think about and with. To the extent that intelligence is a hardware property, one is pretty much stuck with one's original equipment, while the software side of intelligence could be acquired by experience, study and practice.

Complementing this software-hardware sense of the mind-brain question is yet another that might be called the window sense. We know certain mind-brain events primarily through the window of our subjective experiences, and only very indirectly and crudely through neurophysiological or other brain-oriented studies. Mental imagery is an example. On the other hand, certain other mind-brain events, let us say the linguistic difficulties of aphasia, we know principally through the window of neurophysiological understanding. Applying the same contrast to intelligence, one can ask whether our understanding of intelligence comes by way of the mind window, the brain window, or both.

The analysis of views of intelligence into power, tactical and knowledge theories helps place intelligence with reference to both these versions of the mind-brain question. Broadly speaking, power theories of intelligence locate intelligence more in brain than in mind. The emphasis on speed and accuracy of processing as a pervasive characteristic of the intelligent person suggests a hardware-level property of the system. Analogously, computer hardware is characterized by cycle time and error rate. Practice has little effect on intelligence; this fact speaks against a power theory for intelligence and suggests that, in general, intelligence behaves like a basic property of the hardware, not modifiable software. As to the window perspective on the mind-brain question, processing speed and accuracy are not straightforwardly parts of our subjective experience of our own minds, as are mental images, articulated positions, deliberate strategies, or evolving plans. But hesitancies, inaccuracies, and gaps of diverse and provocative sorts appear under conditions of brain damage, where there is often a striking sense of a damaged mechanism, a machine gone awry in some mechanical way quite uncharacteristic of mind as we experience it (Gardner 1975).

Just the opposite argument applies to tactical and knowledge theories of intelligence. Plainly learned, both tactics and knowledge count as software. Furthermore, we often have direct subjective experience of the tactics we deploy and the knowledge we exercise: we hold them in mind, regard them, and wield them much as one might wield a screwdriver in one's hand. Of course, by no means does all of our tactics or knowledge allow conscious introspection; a good deal of it operates in an automatized way that makes such inspection difficult, indirect, and unreliable (Nisbett and Wilson 1977). Nonetheless, much of it we can readily pull into our conscious minds, and the rest of it does not seem very different in character, only in accessibility. In fact, often what is now unconscious and inaccessible to ready inspection was once explicit and subject to examination.

In contrast, brain studies do little to illuminate the landscape of tactics and knowledge that figures so prominently in mind. To be sure, there are broad findings, such as that frontal lobe damage impairs the human capacity for planning and intentional behavior (Pribram and Luria 1973). Mathematical expertise, according to recent studies, bears a relation to the concentration of testosterone in prenatal development, which seemingly affects the development of the nervous system (Kolata 1983). But such glimpses through the brain window only inform us about tactics and knowledge in the broadest possible terms, indeed in terms just as interpretable on a power theory. No correlation rule relating particular characteristics of brain to particular tactics and knowledge has appeared, nor would one expect so fine-grained a rule.

In summary, a web of associations makes a power view of intelligence brain-oriented, and tactical and knowledge views of intelligence mind-oriented. All that need be done to settle the "Where is intelligence?" question is to decide which sort of theory is right. Here the trouble begins. First of all, it's difficult to exclude any of the three. If one considers the work of Jensen and others, a power view of intelligence almost certainly has bearing on human intellectual competence. By the same token, a variety of findings speaks plainly to the relevance of tactics and knowledge in intellectual competence. Nor are the arguments by which one view challenges another airtight. For instance, although retardates may differ from normal individuals primarily in neglecting certain metacognitive strategies, the fact remains that the normal individuals learn or discover those strategies while the retardates do not: something other than tactics has to account for that shortfall to avoid an infinite regress in the argument, and this might be g, as Baron (1978) points out.

If not a matter of eliminating options, the problem becomes one of prioritizing or perhaps statistical weighting. An appeal to epistemic priorities does not help much, since the appeal can cut either way. The organic substrate of intelligence, the brain, has genetic and developmental precedence, so one might consider it the seat of true intelligence. On the other hand, the point has often been made that the distinctive character of human civilization reflects not our organic endowment per se, but rather social evolution, by which succeeding generations pass along their accumulated knowledge and wisdom. By this argument, the mind-oriented tactical and knowledge perspectives on intelligence deserve priority.

Lacking a resolution by priorities, one might turn to statistical techniques and seek numerical weightings. Of course, I am not proposing power plus tactics plus knowledge as a "serious" breakdown of intelligence into factors, analogous to the Cattell-Horn theory of fluid versus crystallized intelligence or related models (Cattell 1963; Horn and Cattell 1966; Gustafsson 1984). Still, a statistical fancy is illuminating here. Suppose we settle on measures of a power component of intelligence (perhaps Jensen's reaction-time task [Jensen 1984]), the tactical component (tests of metacognition), and the knowledge component (knowledge-oriented tests in one or more fields). We also select a measure of intellectual competence in general or in some field. We can then gather data from a diverse population, conduct a multiple linear regression, and compute weights for each of the three components to reveal which wields the most influence.

The trouble is that one can forecast the ambiguous results of this statistical solution: all will depend on the choice of a measure of intellectual competence. Suppose, for example, that you are interested in mathematical problem solving, so you make that the criterion. Very likely you will find that the heaviest weight goes to mathematical knowledge and mathematically oriented, but not necessarily general, tactics. For best performance at any point in time in a specific field, knowledge counts more than anything else. To make the point blatantly, whom would you rather have repair your car: a mechanic with a normal IQ and twenty years of experience or a mechanic with an IQ of 200 and no experience?

Suppose instead you choose as your criterion of intellectual competence performance averaged over a diversity of tasks, none of them very like those measured by the knowledge component of your theory of intelligence. Then you will find that the power and tactical components receive the most weight. In still another study, you take as your criterion learning gains over four years of instruction, starting with youngsters who do not have much of a tactical repertoire. You will probably find that the power component of intelligence weighs most heavily. Then again, suppose you ask not what measure predicts gains before several years of study, but what measure explains variance in gains after the years of study. It will be knowledge, principally, because this comes closest to the character of the achievement tests you use to measure the gains. Or if you ask what measure accounts for gains in the handling of unfamiliar problems after a period of instruction, it will be tactics.

So the circumstances allow no clean answer to the question "Where is intelligence—in mind or brain?" Curiously enough, although the mind-brain distinction might seem vague, the confusion does not arise there. The three aspects of intelligence reviewed ally themselves fairly clearly with mind or brain. Rather, it is the concept of intelligence that turns out to be crucially ambiguous. We can have our answer—mind or brain or a proportional mix—only if we commit ourselves to a criterion of intellectual competence, so that we can calculate the contribution from power, tactics, and knowledge. However, it's not clear why one would want to make such a commitment, given that several ways of construing intellectual competence seem to have their advantages for different purposes.

What Is Creativity?

If intelligence is a multiple and often muddled concept, the same holds twice over for creativity. One of the most pernicious confusions about creativity confounds the trait with striking talent. The source of the mix-up is clear enough: many remarkably creative individuals also displayed prodigious talent early in life, Mozart being a well-known example. But dramatic cases are not necessarily typical; much less do they demonstrate a firm rule. Many individuals we regard as highly creative made no such early showing, and talent per se by no means guarantees creativity. An academically or musically talented person can easily develop into no more than a superb technician with little imagination. In short, common experience suggests that early talent is neither a necessary nor a sufficient condition for creativity.

With this caution about what creativity is not, there remains the question of what it is. In prior writings, I have discussed creativity in depth (Perkins 1981) and recently introduced an integrated model of creativity called the snowflake model (Perkins 1984). The model locates creativity in six traits that in combination impart creativity. A creative person need not possess all six traits, and in fact many do not. But, roughly speaking, the more of these traits the person has, the more creative the person. The traits are substantiated by evidence from a variety of sources which I will mention only occasionally here (Perkins 1984).

Creativity depends on aesthetic as much as practical standards. This precept seems plain enough for artistic creativity. Less apparent may be its application to such different worlds of invention as engineering, the sciences, and business. In all those contexts, however, creative people tend to value and invent ideas that are fresh, parsimonious, elegant, powerful, or deep. Such properties constitute a kind of general aesthetic for creativity. They have their practical side, of course. Powerful ideas show their power in improved performance; parsimonious ideas may be parsimonious partly in yielding efficiency and saving money. But a mind-set alert to qualities like power or parsimony sees ideas in terms transcending their short-term payoffs; this helps to keep the creative person free from parochial pressures (Helson 1971; Mansfield and Busse 1981; Pelz and Andrews 1966; Roe 1952a, 1952b; 1963; Perkins 1981).

Creativity depends on attention to purposes as much as results. One image of inventive people styles them as clever problem solvers. Research on both artists and scientists suggests that this picture underplays the role of *problem finding* (Getzels and Csikszentmihalyi 1976; Perkins 1981). Creative people have a flair for asking the right question, not just for finding the right answer. Partly, this is a straightforward matter of allocation of effort. The characteristic pattern of creative thinking includes substantial time devoted to contemplating the nature of the problem, exploring reformulations or transformations of it, or ranging over contexts and circumstances within a field in search of provocative problems and opportunities. In contrast, less creative thinking is solution-oriented. Little time is spent on searching for, selecting, representing, or transforming a problem, as the problem solver accepts the problem as given, inevitable, and clear and moves as swiftly as possible toward a solution.

Creativity depends on mobility more than fluency. A recent tradition of psychological research attempted to locate creativity in capacities called ideational fluency and flexibility. Roughly speaking, these terms refer to a person's ability to generate many varied ideas on a given theme in a short period of time. Such measures of production rate have a prima facie association with creativity, requiring a person to create rapidly on call. However plausible they seem, however, research seeking to relate creativity as gauged by fluency and flexibility measures to creativity as appraised biographically on the basis of real achievement has shown little connection between the two (Crockenberg 1972; Mansfield and Busse 1981; Wallach 1976a, 1976b). Apparently the usual formal measures of fluency and flexibility are too narrow to reflect much of real-world creativity. At the same time, the fundamental insight they exemplify, if not exhaust, has to be recognized: plainly, creativity must have something to do with being able to take alternative viewpoints, generate different perspectives, transform problems in unexpected ways, and so on. To say as much is to appeal not to psychology but logic: by definition, creativity involves such things. *Mobility* serves as a handy term for this feature of creative thinking, a term that avoids commitment to formal measures of fluency and flexibility.

Creativity depends on working at the edge more than the center of one's competence. This holds in several senses. Most simply, notably creative individuals almost invariably are hard workers; they invest in their pursuits the kind of time and effort many individuals would consider unreasonable (Roe 1952b; Perkins 1981, Chapter 8). Time and effort aside, creative individuals stand ready to take risks in pursuit of their endeavors. One of those risks is simply the risk of failure: creative people may attempt projects they are not at all sure they can carry off. It's important to add that functioning at the edge of one's competence is a pattern of conduct considerably broader than creativity. Most high-achieving individuals in any field, creative or not, work close to the edge of their competence. Consider, for example, champion athletes, who have no need to exhibit inventive thinking but routinely, in both competition and day-to-day training, push themselves to their limits.

Creativity depends on being objective as much as subjective. The popular image of the creative person as a self-absorbed loner demands some such remark. Loner he or she may sometimes be, but the loner had better have an objective eye for what is valid, even if others have some catching up to do to see the validity in it. Having that objective eye involves more than being right by luck or talent; it involves reaching for objectivity by such means as looking twice or three times rather than once, putting aside one's ego, seeking advice from trusted colleagues, and testing one's ideas in practice, as in scientific experiments or marketplace settings. For those who wish to protect themselves and their ideas from editorial input, there are many ways to lead a solipsistic life, but such a style is not characteristic of the creative person (Perkins 1981, Chapter 4).

Creativity depends on intrinsic motivation more than extrinsic motivation. A basic and important finding in several studies of motivation and creativity is that intrinsic motivation fuels creative achievement, while extrinsic motivation undermines intrinsic motivation in many, although perhaps not all, creative individuals (Amabile 1983). The intrinsic involvement of a creative artist or scientist in a field shows up in many ways: avowed dedication, long hours, concern with the craft, involvement with ideas, and most straightforwardly resistance to distraction by extrinsic rewards such as higher income for a less creative kind of work. Indeed, intrinsic motivation wields its influence even in blatantly monetary contexts, where the committed and creative mogul often seems to be in it more for the game than the yachts and swimming pools that money can buy.

With the six characteristics of creativity recounted, two points invite emphasis. First of all, the traits are best thought of not in terms of their titles, such as "attention to aesthetics," but with their particular elaborations in mind—for instance, under aesthetics, commitment to ideas that are fresh, parsimonious, elegant, powerful, deep. It is not just *any* aesthetic that drives the creative individual, but one that highlights aspects of originality and reach. Similar remarks apply to the other five traits. Second, lest there be any doubt, the claim is not just that these traits correlate with creativity but that they cause creativity. We often think of creativity as a unitary ability. The present view holds, on the contrary, that creativity emerges from a number of contributing characteristics.

In short, I propose that the six characteristics discussed are the very stuff of creativity. If there is something more, it is simply another characteristic, like the six discussed—not crucial in itself but contributory—that has evaded the present analysis. If the six do not seem soulful or mysterious enough to account for creativity, we have to remember not to mix up the roles of explanation and poetic expression. The analysis of a phenomenon need not feel like our subjective sense of the phenomenon to be a sound analysis of it. Newton's laws do not feel like the wheeling of the planets, but account for their gyrations nonetheless; and Einstein supposedly has warned that it is not the job of a chemical analysis of a cup of tea to taste like the tea.

Creativity as Intelligence with an Accent

The map of creativity outlined above and the map of intelligence proposed earlier must have some relationship, but what? One kind of answer examines the relationship between IQ and creativity. This is a well-studied theme. The answer, at least to a first approximation, is that within a field of expertise very little connection appears (Barron 1969; Wallach 1976a, 1976b). In fact, IQ does not relate strongly to professional performance generally, creative or not. Among physicists or salespersons, the correlations between measures of professional performance and measures of IQ tend to be low. On the other hand, the average IQ of physicists is much higher than the average IQ of salespersons. The usual interpretation of the circumstances is that different professions have rough "entry-level" IQs associated with them. People simply do not become physicists unless they have IQs of perhaps 130 or better; those with lower IQs get filtered out of the academic track that leads to being a physicist. But, given enough intelligence to handle the academic side of a field, a person has nearly as much chance as a colleague of higher IQ to make a creative contribution.

Interesting as far as it goes, this answer does not explain why creativity should vary independently of intelligence within a profession. Nor does it take account of the very broad way of construing intelligence as intellectual competence, which was introduced earlier. IQ records only one aspect of such competence.

Broadly speaking, and correlational results for IQ notwithstanding, intelligence *has* to be related to creativity: to perform creatively is plainly to display a kind of intellectual competence. At the same time, creativity plainly involves more than intellectual competence in general, because many people of high intellectual competence, who for instance do superbly in school, show little imagination. One might say that creativity is intellectual competence of a certain style or used with a certain style. Creativity is intelligence with a creative accent.

A close look at the six characteristics of creativity supports such a reading. For one thing, creativity has a strong motivational color. As discussed, creativity tends to involve an aesthetic orientation, intrinsic motivation concerning the activity in question, the boldness to work at the edge of one's competence, the distance to be objective. None of these constitutes a part of intellectual competence because they are not abilities. But plainly they influence how one deploys what intelligence one has. A person with the same intelligence as someone else but with a contrary motivational profile will pursue projects for extrinsic reasons alone, pay little heed to aesthetics, function safely inside boundaries of competence, and lack distance from circumstances, all of this far from a creative pattern of behavior.

Other aspects of creativity more straightforwardly relate to abilities, although they have their motivational side as well. Attention to purposes as much as results plausibly involves elements of power, tactics, and knowledge as distinguished earlier. As to power, purposes are more abstract and remote from reality than results, and their mental representations consequently more tenuous and less elaborated; the ready manipulation of intensional representations might well benefit from power factors in intelligence. As to tactics, attention to purposes most straightforwardly involves an allocation of resources strategy: more so than a less creative person, a more creative person invests time in activities like searching for problems and opportunities, formulating them, and transforming them. As to knowledge, knowing what makes a good problem or opportunity in a given field usually requires an intimate acquaintance with the field.

Much the same tale can be told for mobility, another characteristic of creativity identified earlier. Mobility might involve power in the form of mental operations of remote association or analogy making, operations with more reach and precision in some people than in others. Likewise, mobility in part could reflect a resource allocation strategy emphasizing attention to transforming problems, seeking new paths, and reaching for relationships. Finally, mobility within a field depends in part on knowing the terrain and the paths it affords. Moreover, such traits as an aesthetic orientation characteristic of creativity or working at the edge of one's competence, although most suggestive of motivational factors, involve intelligence as well. To respond aesthetically to parsimony or originality, one must be able to perceive it; to work at the edge of one's competence, one must be able to hold in mind and manipulate the complex, ambiguous, and fluctuating mental representations likely to inhabit that insecure borderland. This, too, plainly might involve power, tactics, and knowledge.

However, it's worth asking which figures crucially in creativity— power, tactics, or knowledge? Arguably, tactics does, but the other two do not. The knowledge that underwrites mobility, attention to purposes, and so on, might well be possessed by individuals of little creativity. The powers that equip one to deal readily with abstract and often ephemeral representations also do nothing in themselves to promote creativity. In contrast, the tactics equipping a person to deal in purposes, exercise mobility, attend to values like originality, and so on, specifically bias a person toward creative behavior. They marshall the power and knowledge of the person in a creative direction. This makes all the more appropriate the notion that creativity is intelligence with an accent. As the motivational profiles of creative people promote the deployment of their powers, tactics, and knowledge to creative ends, so do the tactical profiles of creative people promote the deployment of their powers and knowledge to creative ends.

The point can be made a little differently as follows. Suppose you want to design a creative person. To ensure an intellectually competent person, you will equip the person with the needed mental powers, appropriate tactics for problem solving in general and in a specialty, and knowledge in the desired specialty. For the creative person you will need to add the tactical and motivational profiles characteristic of creativity. These will orient the person toward the creative use of his or her powers, other tactics, and knowledge. So again, creativity is intelligence with a certain accent.

Creativity in Mind and Brain

Where is creativity—in mind or brain? By this point in the inquiry, several tools that might help with an answer are at hand. As discussed earlier, the mind-body sense of the question is uninteresting in this context. But the hardware-software and mind window versus brain window senses of the question might yield more provocative answers. Also, the relationships among intelligence, mind and brain, and the relation of creativity to intelligence have already been examined. What picture results?

In its link to intelligence, creativity is a property of mind. Power, tactics, and knowledge all play a role in creative thought, as just discussed; but of the three, tactics uniquely biases a person toward creativity. It was decided earlier that tactics are more a part of mind than of brain, making the link between creativity and intelligence more a matter of mind than brain in both the software-hardware and window senses.

But the motivational profile of the creative individual remains to be reckoned with. How does this sort between mind and brain? Let us take the window sense of the question first. To be sure, brain figures in our emotional lives in some partially understood ways. Distinctive and encompassing motivations and emotions such as passion, hunger, or rage may be evoked by direct stimulation of the brain or by tumors or other insults to the thinking organ. The problem is that motivation as seen through the brain window appears in broad strokes, without the detail characteristic of such matters as aesthetic responses, intrinsic motivation, or navigating at the edge of one's competence. The mind window, however, offers us through our experiences of ourselves a more nuanced view. The motivational side of creativity is better seen through mind than brain.

The software-hardware sense of the mind-brain question does not yield so easy an answer. It's not clear to what extent the motivational pattern characteristic of creativity is learned. To be sure, to some extent it very likely is. For instance, autonomy and self-reliance, which are apparently related to creativity, are fostered by complex environments that engage the organism in frequent decision making, more than by simple environments that do not (Schooler 1984). On the other hand, personality characteristics to some extent may be inborn and not so malleable. Thus, one can say that creativity tends toward being a property of mind, but one must also remember the in-between and ill-defined status of motivation as it pertains to the software-hardware sense of the question.

Another reservation perhaps counts for even more: the peculiarly futile quality of spending so much thought trying to sort out creativity between brain and mind. In a deep sense, a decision like that cannot be terribly interesting. It suffers from the same problem of informational sparseness that plagues the popular research on right-brain versus left-brain functions. Even if we get a clean answer, we still do not have very much information about what's going on. Right versus left represents only one binary unit of information—one bit—and one bit is as little information as you can have about anything. Imagine a young geographer inquiring whether London lies in the northern or southern hemisphere, or a young biologist asking whether a platypus is a plant or an animal, and you get a sense of how hollow a simple answer to the mind-brain question is.

But if the answer is not so interesting, the reasons for it are. In arguing out how creativity and intelligence map into mind and brain, and how the two relate to one another, we end up knowing the whole terrain better in worthwhile ways. We understand, for instance, why the mind window yields a better picture of creativity than the brain window: creativity is a relatively particular and nuanced human trait, one that at our current state of knowledge does not show through the somewhat blurry brain window. We see that whatever limitations exist on power theories of intelligence, the tactical and knowledge dimensions of intelligence offer opportunities for improvement. Creativity invites our efforts to marshall and wield it, encourage and expand it, working through the tactical and motivational profiles characteristic of it. For mere whimsy you might teach yourself to talk in a Maine or Texas accent. But to put your mind to better use, you might help yourself and those around you to think with a creative accent.

References

Amabile, T. 1983. *The Social Psychology of Creativity*. New York: Springer-Verlag.

Baron, J. 1978. "Intelligence and General Strategies." *Strategies in information processing*, pp. 28–40. Edited by G. Underwood. London: Academic Press.

Barron, F. 1969. *Creative Person and Creative Process*. New York: Holt, Rinehart, & Winston.

Cattell, R. 1963. "Theory of Fluid and Crystallized Intelligence: A Critical Experiment." *Journal of Educational Psychology* 54:1–22.

Chase, W. and Simon, H. 1973. "Perception in Chess." *Cognitive Psychology* 4:55–81.

Chi, M., Feltovich, P., and Glaser, R. 1981. "Categorization and Representation of Physics Problems by Experts and Novices." *Cognitive Science* 5:121–152.

Crockenberg, S. 1972. "Creativity Tests: A Boon or Boondoggle for Education?" *Review of Educational Research* 42:27–45.

Gardner, H. 1975. *The Shattered Mind*. New York: Knopf.

Gardner, H. 1983. *Frames of Mind*. New York: Basic Books.

Getzels, J. and Csikszentmihalyi, M. 1976. *The Creative Vision: A Longitudinal Study of Problem Finding in Art*. New York: John Wiley & Sons.

de Groot, A. 1965. *Thought and Choice in Chess*. The Hague: Mouton.

Guilford, J. 1967. *The Nature of Human Intelligence*. New York: McGraw-Hill.

Guilford, J. and Hoepfner, R. 1971. *The Analysis of Intelligence.* New York: McGraw-Hill.

Gustafsson, J. 1984. "A Unifying Model for the Structure of Intellectual Abilities." *Intelligence* 8:179–203.

Helson, R. 1971. "Women Mathematicians and the Creative Personality." *Journal of Consulting and Clinical Psychology* 36:210–220.

Horn, J. and Cattell, R. 1966. "Refinement and Test of the Theory of Fluid and Crystallized Intelligence." *Journal of Educational Psychology* 57:253–270.

Horn, J. and Knapp, J. 1973. "On the Subjective Character of the Empirical Base of Guilford's Structure of Intellect Model." *Psychological Bulletin* 80:33–43.

Jensen, A. 1984. "Test Validity: g versus the Specificity Doctrine." *Journal of Social and Biological Structure* 7:93–118.

Kolata, G. 1983. "Math Genius May Have a Hormonal Basis." *Science* 222:1312.

Larkin, J., McDermott, J., Simon, D., and Simon, H. 1980. "Modes of Competence in Solving Physics Problems." *Cognitive Science* 4:317–345.

Longstreth, L. 1984. "Jensen's Reaction-time Investigations of Intelligence: A Critique." *Intelligence* 8:139–160.

Mansfield, R. and Busse, T. 1981. *The Psychology of Creativity and Discovery.* Chicago: Nelson-Hall.

Nisbett, R. and Wilson, T. 1977. "Telling More Than We Can Know: Verbal Reports on Mental Process." *Psychological Review* 84:231–259.

Pelz, D. and Andrews, F. 1966. *Scientists in Organizations: Productive Climates for Research and Development.* New York: John Wiley & Sons.

Perkins, D. 1981. *The Mind's Best Work.* Cambridge, Mass.: Harvard University Press.

Perkins, D. 1984. "Creativity by Design." *Educational Leadership* 42:18–25.

Polya, G. 1954. *Mathematics and Plausible Reasoning.* 2 vols. Princeton, N.J.: Princeton University Press.

Polya, G. 1957. *How to Solve It: A New Aspect of Mathematical Method.* 2nd ed. Garden City, N.Y.: Doubleday.

Pribram, K. and Luria, A., eds. 1973. *Psychophysiology of the Frontal Lobes.* New York: Academic Press.

Roe, A. 1952a. "A Psychologist Examines Sixty-four Eminent Scientists." *Scientific American* 187:21–25.

Roe, A. 1952b. *The Making of a Scientist.* New York: Dodd, Mead & Co.

Roe, A. 1963. "Psychological Approaches to Creativity in Science." *Essays on Creativity in the Sciences*, pp. 153–182. Edited by M. A. Coler. New York: New York University.

Schoenfeld, A. 1980. "Teaching Problem-solving Skills." *American Mathematical Monthly* 87:794–805.

Schoenfeld, A. 1982. "Measures of Problem-solving Performance and of Problem-solving Instruction." *Journal for Research in Mathematics Education* 13:31–49.

Schoenfeld, A. and Herrmann, D. 1982. "Problem Perception and Knowledge Structure in Expert and Novice Mathematical Problem Solvers." *Journal of Experimental Psychology: Learning, Memory, and Cognition* 8:484–494.

Schooler, C. 1984. "Psychological Effects of Complex Environments during the Life Span: A Review and Theory." *Intelligence* 8:259–281.

Soloway, E. and Ehrlich, K. 1984. "Empirical Studies of Programming Knowledge." *IEEE Transactions on Software Engineering* SE-10 : 595 – 609.

Sternberg, R. 1977. *Intelligence, Information Processing, and Analogical Reasoning: The Componential Analysis of Human Abilities.* New York: John Wiley & Sons.

Wallach, M. 1976a. "Psychology of Talent and Graduate Education." *Individuality in Learning*, pp. 178 – 210. Edited by S. Messick and Associates. San Francisco: Jossey-Bass.

Wallach, M. 1976b. "Tests Tell Us Little About Talent." *American Scientist* 64 : 57 – 63.

Wickelgren, W. 1974. *How to Solve Problems: Elements of a Theory of Problems and Problem Solving.* San Francisco: W. H. Freeman and Co.

The Literary Imagination

Doris Grumbach

My earliest idea about the brain was formed in the nursery. I was told by my mother that my head was filled by what she called grey matter. That seemed to me to be a dead, dingy, and derogatory description for my head, which I had pictured as full of flashing light and color, like a Catherine wheel or a Roman candle. Later in college I learned some details about that grey matter. On a bet, I studied neuro-anatomy in my senior year, forty-five years ago. My roommate was a premedical student, I a philosophy major. In our junior year I was elected to Phi Beta Kappa and she, far brighter than I, was not. Her theory was that if she had taken all the soft literature and philosophy courses that I had she too would have been elected to what the college president called, at the induction, the fraternity of the intellect. So I took one of her courses to prove her wrong, a course that attempted to explain the brain to me. What I learned was something about the enormous complexity of that organ, and a few wonderful words: cerebrum, cerebellum, thalamus, hypothalamus, and medulla oblongata, those lovely denotative nominatives which, to me, had the very ring of chant and poetry.

Because I could see before me in the laboratory the parts of the brain, I began to think of the mind as a miasma, an ineffable haze surrounding the locatable core that was the brain. I knew the brain was the control and command center, that orders for actions emanated from it, commands to perform in some way or cease to perform. What, where, were ideas, concepts, connections, epiphanies, realizations, recognitions? Where did they come from, what was their locale? By what mysterious agency did the contents of the fog-mind arrive, often unbidden and unplanned for, it seemed, to the pen?

To this day, fifty years after I lost the bet to my college friend because I did badly in the course, I am still puzzled about everything that emanates from the brain through the mysterious fog, the mind, surrounding it (to my uninformed view of things) and thence to my pen. Every day at my desk, working on fiction and criticism, the miracle occurs, unexplainable by logic. The idea arrives in some unexplainable way, from some undiscovered country. By what afferent pathway comes the image, the simile, the connection, the metaphor, the symbol that clarifies in an almost epiphanic flash the murkiness of my muddy prose, turning it into sense and even, sometimes, illumination?

My theories about this mystery have tended to be wild. If I were not addressing persons far more educated than I in the intricacies of neuroanatomy and physiology, psychology, and psychiatry, I would offer my truly vulgar explanation of how I now see the mind of the artist. Well, despite the elevation of my readers, I will do so nevertheless. To my imagistic way of thinking, the mind is a compost heap, composed of everything one has heard, overheard, seen, imagined, dreamed, been told, read, remembered. The richer the organic matter dumped into the pile, the more the terrible roil works, the more odorous and interesting are the emanations from it, the better the effluvia that rise up and out of it. The mind, this compost heap, is fertilized and then becomes to the fiction fertilizing. That successful fiction or poetry comes to the pen (or to the typewriter, or, god help us, to the word processor and computer) is, I believe, the result of the extraordinary richness in that unique and irreplaceable, unduplicatable hoard.

All this I see as a closed system of rich cause and enriched effect. But the mind is sometimes nudged into action by something that occurs outside, much like the way a sea anemone responds to the intrusion of a finger or a stick or a natural enemy. Henry James calls these outside stimuli "germs" and says that his stories begin from or are caused by "a precious particle," "a single small seed," "a casual hint," "a mere particle floating in the stream of talk" of a neighbor, as in the case of *The Spoils of Poynton*. James describes the prodding process in this way:

Such is the interesting truth about the stray suggestion, the wandering word, the vague echo, at touch of which the novelist's imagination winces as at the prick of some sharp point: its virtue is all in its needle-like quality, the power to penetrate as finely as possible. This fineness it is that communicates the virus of suggestion, any thing more than the minimum of which spoils the operation. If one is given a hint at all designedly one is sure to be given too much; one's subject is in the merest grain, the speck of truth, of beauty, of reality, scarce visible to the common eye—since, I firmly hold, a good eye for a subject is anything but usual. Strange and attaching, certainly, the consistency with which the first thing to be done for the communicated and seized idea is to reduce almost to nought the form, the air as of a mere disjoined and lacerated lump of life, in which we may have happened to meet it. (James 1945)

The sensitivity and receptiveness of that composted agglommeration I have called the mind, the artist's "mind's eye," as the expression goes, or his imagination, as James terms it, welcomes the germ, the precious particle, and permits it to root, gives it *lebensraum*. The subsequent selectivity and discrimination of the writer's craft result in the ruthless elimination of some of its roots and offshoots in order for the "tiny nugget," as James calls it, to stand clear and to appear to the reader to be entirely right, "washed free of awkward accretions and hammered into a sacred hardness," which is form. There is to life itself, James points out, a sense of "splendid waste"; to art there is only order and harmony, the result of the action of craft upon the disorder, even chaos, that life presents to us. The craft of the artist excludes the confusion of life, and puts as Paul Valéry says, "a restraint on chance." (I hope you will excuse my method here. I have used as authority the poets Paul Valéry and Samuel Taylor Coleridge and novelists Henry James and John Gardner, because it seemed to me that writers who testify to their experience are the best source of the imprecise experience we are trying to put our hands on.)

There are, of course, many explanations for how the literary mind functions when it begins to write. Paul Valéry saw the poet as an extraordinary receptacle. "The poet at work is an expectation," he writes in *The Art of Poetry* (Valéry 1958, p. 174). "We wait for the unexpected word which cannot be foreseen but must be awaited." The poet is the first to hear it, "his ear speaks to him, he is offered the germ [here Valéry echoes James's word], which may be no more than a word or a fragment of a sentence, a line that seeks and toils to create its own justification and so gives rise to a context, a subject. . . ."

The seed, the germ, arrives from the outside by luck or chance, but it falls on receptive ground that is the hypersensitive mind of the writer. The process so described is sometimes called inspiration, a far more elevated and elegant concept than my uncouth idea of the compost heap. Inspiration has a theological connotation, stemming from the Middle English word *inspirin* meaning to breathe in. In the language we still retain the word *inspirit*, meaning to animate, to fill with spirit. Some creative persons speak of inspiration as the mysterious and fortunate source of their work, unaware of the religious implications of the word: for fifty days after Easter, the Gospel of Saint John informs us, the Holy Spirit descended upon and entered into the Apostles, Jesus having breathed into them. Acts 2 has a more dramatic account: "And suddenly a sound came from Heaven like the rush of a mighty wind and it filled all the house where they were sitting. . . . And there appeared to them tongues of fire . . . and they were all filled with the Holy Spirit and began to speak in tongues as the Spirit gave them utterance."

This view of inspiration in its theological implications is not one that writers generally hold when they speak of inspiration, but in essence they agree that what they experience has a mysterious and unaccountable source which the Gospels call the Holy Spirit, but which they think of as something less spectral, more mundane, much more like the roaring of the highly ideational wind filling the house of the writer's mind and granting him, *mirabile dictu*, a tongue of fire.

Personally I can accept John's Gospel, because I am so overwhelmed by what I have been given during the cryptic and enigmatic process. The mind of the writer might be charted if one could know everything that went into it since the first conscious moment, but the germ, the precious article often comes to one serendipitously, a gift of fortune. True, it falls upon a place designed, developed, and formed to receive it. Paul Valéry speaks of passing "from an impure form, a mixture of all the resources of the mind to a pure form that is, one solely verbal and organized . . ." (Valéry 1958, p. 178). Sometimes "inspiration," if we decide to use that suspicious word (to some), resides in another attribute of the creative imagination we hear assigned to the artist: intuition, a gift Nature or God bestows on the intensely aware and sensitive person. Valéry believes the poet has "essentially the intuition of a special order of combinations. A certain combination of objects (of thoughts) which has no value for a normal man has for him an existence and makes itself noticed" (Valéry 1958, p. 181).

To my uninstructed way of thinking, what Valéry calls intuition is the highly developed, if unsummoned and uncalled for, ability of the mind to understand the invisible, arising out of a myriad of materials that have fertilized the mind/compost heap, an unusual suggestibility and sensibility that develops as a result of all the forced feeding of the heap over so many years; so that connections and combinations, yes, and revelations that arrive on the page, I have heard it claimed, are not so much the result of intuition or inspiration but explainable to a degree if the contents of the mind's aggregation had been recorded since birth in some computerized way as they arrived from their multiple sources. Stored there and awaiting the retrieval, the matter that results in art might be explained by these sources, by the combinations and mixtures of these sources, and by the learned or instinctive craft with which they are captured and used. The fanciful artist may call what results revelation. The scientist will shudder at the word.

The climate, the weather, of creation is, I suspect, what Valéry calls "a special disturbance" in the mind, a curious stirring of the stored matter, sometimes coming about with hurricane suddenness, and sometimes during the becalmed state characteristic of contemplation in which all artists indulge, according to Evelyn Underhill in her study called *Mysticism* (1955). After this disturbance, Valéry says, "a certain harmony" takes possession of the artist, "between our inner physical and psychic disposition and the circumstances (real or imaginary) that impress us." It may be this climate during the process of creation that suggested to the late John Gardner the parallel between writing fiction and dreaming. This observation, which equates art and one of the ordinary states of consciousness, explains as well the reader's state when he accepts what Gardner calls "the dream of fiction," an abnegation of the known real, an acceptance of the dream state of the unreal or fictional. Valéry too sees a parallel between the universe of dream and the poetic (that is, creative) state. A dream makes us see in a common and frequent experience how our consciousness can be invaded, filled up, composed. In much the same way the state in which fiction is composed begins, develops, and dissolves within us. It is wholly irregular, inconstant, involuntary, fragile and we lose it, as we acquire it, by accident.

For the writer of fiction and poetry the mode and pathway to his art is language. In the beginning was the word, says the Gospel writer John, and for the creative writer it is the same. The writer creates a world composed entirely of words (what else indeed is there for him?). The source, the supply, the choice, the co-mission as well as the omission involved in the choice of words, are entirely within himself. Through words the writer knows himself; through words he advances into exploration of other persons and other things. Language—its sound, its denotative and connotative meanings, its etymology as well as the private association of meaning everyone has for important words—is the message and the medium, the tool and the bench, the vision and the dream, the alpha and omega of written creation. The word represents, for the writer, the truth, so that fiction which works takes on all the lineaments of truth, is true in the curious way that the created becomes the truth. In a letter that Gustave Flaubert wrote to his mistress, Louise Colet, in 1853 he says, "Everything you invent is true; you can be sure of that." And in *Ironweed*, a recent novel by William Kennedy, the noble bum Francis Phelan is talking to his side-kick Rudy. Rudy says:

> "Where'd you get them clothes?"
> "Found 'em."
> "Found 'em? Where'd you find 'em?"
> "Up a tree."
> "A tree?"
> "Yeah. A tree. Grew everything. Suits, shoes, bow ties."
> "You never tell me nothin' that's true."
> "Hell, it's all true," Francis said. "Every stinkin' damn thing you can think of is true." (Kennedy 1983)

Flaubert and Kennedy are not, of course, talking about scientific or mathematical truth, verifiable and demonstrable, but fictional truth which is receivable and acceptable revelation about the human condition, something we recognize as consistent with our own views of the ways in which human beings think and live. What is truest of all, to the fiction writer, is that "every stinkin' thing is true."

Grouped into configurations, words are the vehicles for images. The success of evocation in poetry and prose depends upon the entire rightness of words. Figurative language is the poet's only evidence of things not seen. Language serves the writer to reveal, of course, what he has seen but also what he is capable of guessing or inventing, and metaphor—that extension of the word into a richer level of suggested meaning—both adds to the power of the simple word and thrusts deep into the mystery of meaning.

The word selected, out of limitless possibilities, and the images the writer forms from boundless available sights, the figures of speech that come to him, empower his vision with new levels of illustration and allusion. All these are the ways the writer makes the already-made, the real—graphic and terrifying—vivid and highly charged with emotion. Penetrating the mysterious matter that is his mind, the writer uses the

sharp instruments of words in all their configurations and then, stab-
bing about like a skilled rapier-wielder, he cuts through the real world,
the "film of familiarity," as Coleridge calls it, revealing "a Nature into
which his own feelings, his aspirations and apprehensions are projected." So he gains some small insight into reality which results not in
reality translated to the page but in an imaginative re-creation of it
which we call fiction and poetry. He has nudged at reality with his instrument, the word, the visible manifestation of his art. The reader sees
what the writer makes him see, feels what the writer requires him to
feel. Emotion rises miraculously from the page, life itself rises from the
page, the dead print and the compressed tree parts that are the page
come alive, the consequence of this complicated initiation and trans-
ference from life to art. In "Peter Quince at the Clavier," Wallace
Stevens writes, "Music is feeling, not sound . . ." (Stevens 1967). In
fiction and poetry the words, primal and the beginning of everything,
end by producing feeling, not meaning alone.

How does the writer feel while he is waiting for the word, the image, the figure of speech, the sentence and then, it having arrived,
when he puts it down? The late John Gardner said he experienced an
"altered sense of things." "In some apparently inexplicable way the
mind opens up: one steps out of the world. . . . One knows one was
away. . . . All writing requires at least some measure of a trancelike
state." And the reader in turn is the recipient of a gift. For all good fiction sets off, in Gardner's terms "a vivid and continuous dream in the
reader's mind" (Gardner 1983).

I have looked at a few possible sources for the creative work, some
stimuli that set these source-matters to work, and the method, the craft
that forms the raw materials into art. I would like to end this highly
speculative exploration by examining a word used often in such discussions: imagination.

In *Biographia Literaria* Coleridge describes imagination as "that synthetic and magical power." He makes no further incursions into a
definition or thoughts about its origin. Only its results occupy his attention. Imagination, he says, reveals itself in "the balance or recon-
ciliation of opposite or discordant qualities . . . the sense of novelty
and freshness with old and familiar objects; a more than usual state of
emotion, with more than usual order." The gifts (and by gifts I take it he
means the results) of imagination are "the sense of musical delight,
with the power of reducing multitude into unity of effect, and modifying a series of thoughts by some one predominant thought or feeling"
(Coleridge 1968).

The creative writer, Coleridge seems to be suggesting, is like the ordinary man in that he has experiences which evoke response. But the creative writer has a far wider field of available stimulation and resources, perhaps (dare I call it here a higher compost heap?), and his responses are more complete. I. A. Richards believes that the ordinary person suppresses nine-tenths of his impulses because he is incapable of managing them without confusion. "He goes about the world in blinkers because what he would otherwise see would upset him. But the poet through his superior power of ordering experience is freed from this necessity" (Richards 1961). Imagination in these descriptions is not an organ but a highly developed magical power, or it is an unusual power that transforms and redeems the world outside, reducing it to affecting charged cognates in the world of fiction and poetry.

At this moment, two footnotes about creativity occur to me, although everything that has gone before is mere footnote. What role does what we call intelligence play in the creative act? Perhaps it is because we do not properly understand its sources that I am tempted to say: almost none. As a child I believed that only good persons wrote good books. I have lived to see the falsity of that. And in the same way, I see that few creative artists are noticeably intelligent. Memory is important to the writer, available, constantly working memory, but the intellect is not usually part of his necessary equipment, often indeed, gets in the way of what he wants to do. The literary critic most often makes a poor novelist or poet. The analytic mind staggers before the mysteries and imponderables of the creative impulse. I seriously doubt the "patterns of effort allocation," as Doctor Perkins puts it, have anything at all to do with it, or will, or motivation which seriously falters all too often.

A second footnote: it has been noticed by novelists like Thomas Mann that the symptoms of physical illness and the symptoms of the creative state bear a close resemblance. The writer works in a fevered way, sometimes unaware of what is coming to his pen. His weakness at the end of a day of work resembles the weakness of sickness. Conversely, the sick often experience states of mind like that of the creative person. I think there is no difficulty about accepting both exceptional and abnormal states of the mind and the body as close to each other.

But more impelling, perhaps, is the suggested alliance between madness and the creative state, particularly the often observed presence of depression, resembling the psychotic state, in the writer. It is true: the poet and the fiction writer are often dogged by depression. Words will not come, nothing that does come works well, the prospect before the writer towers, but his ability to scale it seems to him inadequate. The writer sits, inert, blocked, unable to put anything down. He doesn't eat or take walks, he drinks to drown his despair, to wipe out the unbridgeable gap between his Platonic view of perfect work and the enormous imperfection of his meager accomplishment. A few take their lives in the face of this disparity. Others are brutal to their wives, cruel to their children, gamble away their resources, sniff cocaine.

Relationships, marriages, friendships, do not easily survive these periods, or the long sessions of seclusion when the writer turns away from everyone but his tormented self in order to battle in isolation the difficulties of his art. Frequent occurrences of these states have led scientists to study creative persons to see if, indeed, their extreme states of mind—depression, irritability, blocked activity—do not parallel the psychotic state. Novelists themselves have been aware of the parallel and have used characters driven by creative madness in their fictions. Freud, of course, believed that art was close to neurosis.

Whatever the resemblance, it seems clear that writers and poets are no more mad or neurotic than persons who do not have their peculiar creative urges: they are merely more eccentric when, as we say, the creative madness is upon them. The nature of their work, the necessary solitude in which the literary imagination operates, the extremes of elation and depression that success or failure engender, the highly personal and often painful journeys into the self that are required (I think of the medieval bestiary which pictures the spider as pulling his web with his front spinnerets from his own chest as an analogy to what the writer does), the technical difficulties of the craft—all these often result in antisocial behavior and apparent, if temporary, personality disorders.

Normal persons dislike living with writers, whom they grow to regard as egocentric, selfish, moody, and unpredictable. They are. And, in addition, they are sometimes alcoholic, neurotic, and often in need of counselling or psychiatric help for their despair. But these traits belong to other segments of the population in some degree or other—to workaholics, academics, actors, students, architects, journalists, parents, ministers, among others. I suspect that the number of writers who have periods of madness in their lives or take their lives is in the same proportion to the number of people writing as the mad and the suicidal are to the general population.

What the researchers into the phenomenon of creativity may have noticed is that, like the madman in his constant absorption with his obsession, the creative writer, as he works, concentrates in an almost obsessive way, and feels himself to be more aware, hypersensitive, elevated by successes and depressed by failures. There is a kind of madness implicit in his method. And what is more, he has a curious sense of being more fully alive than in his ordinary life, a sense much like, it seems to me, what one feels at the moment of falling in love. I recall an adolescent daughter of mine who once combined these elements. She said she had fallen in love with a fourteen-year-old boy, a year her senior. She talked about him constantly at table, beginning every sentence with "John said." My husband and I stood it for a while, but when her sentences started to begin with "John's mother said," I had enough. I said to her: "Barbie, this is silly. You don't know anything about love. This is puppy-love, and I'm sick of it. I don't want to hear anything more about it." She fixed me with that look that teenaged daughters give their mothers and said, "Mother, didn't you feel this way when you were alive?"

So. Having come this long way through possible sources, stimuli, states of mind, and parallels in illness and psychosis, I come to the moral of my daughter's question applied to creativity. Like love and passion, the creative imagination when it is working well is perhaps more alive, in a greater state of expectancy, than is the mind in its normal state. From this privileged condition—inspired, if you will—come poetry and fictional prose of a high order. In turn, this good work provides readers with heightened emotion, understanding, and insight, with the sense that they are better, wiser, and more aware, yes and more alive, for having entered the writer's unique world, closer to the natural world and the unnatural world of men. As for the writer, he is everlastingly grateful for whatever arrives, or is given to him, from whatever source, serendipitous or determined, from the mystery of the mind or the greater mystery of inspiration. With the poet Gerard Manley Hopkins, in "Pied Beauty," the writer thanks God or whatever powers may be for

> All things counter, original, spare, strange;
> Whatever is fickle, freckled (who knows how?)
> With swift, slow; sweet, sour; adazzle, dim;
> He fathers-forth whose beauty is past change:
> Praise him. (Hopkins 1967)

Finally: I trust you will take all that I have said, not as an approach that features logic, reason, scientific analysis, research, probable hypothesis, but rather as one long, extended metaphor, or if you prefer, as an ode or an elegy, a lyric, a sonnet of speculative ramblings—in other words, pure, unadulterated poetry. Is it true? Hardly, in one sense. Is it all a lie? Perhaps.

References

Coleridge, S. 1968. *Biographia Literaria*. Edited by J. Shawcross. Oxford: Oxford University Press.

Gardner, J. 1983. *On Becoming a Novelist*. New York: Harper and Row.

Hopkins, G. 1967. "Pied Beauty." *The Poems of Gerard Manley Hopkins*. 4th ed. Edited by W. H. Gardner and N. H. Mackenzie. New York: Oxford University Press.

James, H. 1945. *The Spoils of Poynton. The Novels and Tales of Henry James*. New York: Scribners.

Kennedy, W. 1983. *Ironweed*. New York: Viking Press.

Richards, I. 1961. *Principles of Literary Criticism*. New York: Harcourt, Brace and World.

Stevens, W. 1967. "Peter Quince at the Klavier." *The Collected Poems of Wallace Stevens*. New York: Alfred Knopf.

Underhill, E. 1955. *Mysticism: A Study in the Nature and Development of Man's Spiritual Consciousness*. Cleveland: World Publishers.

Valéry, P. 1958. *The Art of Poetry*. XLV Bollingen Series. New York: Pantheon.

Are Minds Developed or Created?

Maxine Greene

From the vantage point of education, there can be no either/or: minds are developed *and* created. Most teachers have learned to take into account the processes of development, variously charted and conceived. Depending on their orientation, they see themselves as stimulating natural processes, nurturing them, or deliberately guiding them. Some have "end-states" in mind, usually having to do with cognitive proficiency. Others take an open-ended view: in a Deweyan mode, they would say that "there is nothing to which growth is relative save more growth, there is nothing to which education is subordinate save more education" (Dewey 1916, p. 60). When it comes to the content of teaching, most teachers recognize the necessity to relate the concepts or subject matters they are attempting to communicate to particular stages or phases of student growth. The very idea of content, however, whether referring to beliefs, ways of behaving, rules, or the symbol systems available for structuring experience, draws attention to the need to take the young beyond where they are.

L. S. Vygotsky says that children's actual development levels define "functions that have already matured, that is the end products of development" (Vygotsky 1978, p. 86). What he calls a "zone of proximal development" has to be considered if we are to find a clue to the understanding of the internal course of development:

By using this method we can take account of not only the cycles and maturation processes that have already been completed but also those processes that are currently in a state of formation, that are just beginning to mature and develop. Thus, the zone of proximal development permits us to delineate the child's immediate future and his dynamic developmental state, allowing not only for what has already been achieved developmentally but also for what is in the course of maturing. (Vygotsky 1978, p. 87)

Learning, social interaction, the asking of questions all help create these zones of proximal development, he writes, and awaken "a variety of internal developmental processes that are able to operate only when a child is interacting with people in his environment and in cooperation with his peers" (Vygotsky 1978, p. 90). Jerome Bruner, in commenting on this, points out that Vygotsky made us realize that what matters is not so much intelligent action as measurable in the here and now, "but the extent to which a person is *instructible* given optimum conditions" (Miller 1983, p. 41). It seems clear enough that the educator, through his or her very vocation, must be interested in what is beginning in the student, what he or she can become in some "immediate future," not so much in what the student has already become.

   John Dewey attributes the "educability" of human beings to "the possibility of continuing diversification of behavior" (Dewey 1960, p. 260). For him, the development of mind involves increasing capacities for "preferential action"; and he consistently tries to transfer the issue "from the past to the future, from antecedents to consequences" (Dewey 1960, p. 264). The educator, then, concerned for the release of preferences and the encouragement of responsible choice, has to devise the kinds of situations that allow for multiple transactions and the kinds of stimulation that provoke young people to become different from what they are. Questioning has to be deliberately encouraged; problems have to be posed; inquiries have to be initiated and carried through. In other words, teachers must concentrate on doing what they can to move students to attend, probe, ponder, imagine, to reach beyond themselves to what is not yet. There is always an element of unpredictability in this kind of teaching-learning situation, since people are being asked to act on their own initiatives, not merely to *behave* in response to predetermined stimuli or commands. All this signifies a bringing of something new into the world on the part of learners empowered to learn to learn. Meanings, perspectives, insights, intuitions, images: if all or any of these have to do with mindfulness, the creation of minds may be seen to go on.

But it would not be a creation through molding or manipulation by outside hands or agencies. Analogues are not to be found in the shaping or creating of works of art, since art-making involves working with material that may be resistant but has no agency of its own. Jean Piaget used to draw attention to the importance of "active methods" when it came to teaching, meaning those that included both individual and cooperative work and that led to "training in self-discipline and voluntary effort" (Gruber and Vonèche 1977, p. 712). And indeed, the notion of voluntariness has become focal in much thinking about educating human minds today. Without it, it would be impossible to talk about learning as a type of action, since action, unlike behavior, signifies the taking of initiatives by people *choosing*, as it were, to explore, to find out, to construct, to renew.

Philosophers with varying standpoints link the growth of mind to such exercising of free will, and to the taking of responsibility. Many place a primary emphasis on what Gilbert Ryle calls an idea "cardinal to the notion of teaching, training, education" (Ryle 1967, p. 105). For him, it is a question of students being taught how to do certain things and then going on to teach themselves. "I give you the *modus operandi*," he writes, "but your operatings or tryings to operate according to this *modus* are your own doings and not my inflictings and the practising by which you master the method is your exertion and not mine" (Ryle 1967, p. 119). Ryle was a British analytic philosopher. Maurice Merleau-Ponty, a French phenomenologist, uses another tone but much the same approach when he writes that what defines the human being is "the capacity of going beyond created structures in order to create others" (Merleau-Ponty 1968, p. 175). Not only does this characterize what existentialists and phenomenologists call consciousness; it describes the creation of mind. It has much to do with the ability to choose and the capacity to take a variety of points of view with respect to what is being done or made or studied. It has to do with "the capacity of orienting oneself in relation to the possible, to the mediate, and not in relation to a limited milieu" (Merleau-Ponty 1968, p. 176).

Because the educational philosopher's interest is largely in *praxis*, or reflected-upon classroom practice, he or she is unlikely to speculate very much about brain-states or some sort of "wiring" that might explain learning and growth. When confronted with retardation or other mental handicaps, of course, educators are inclined to look for neurophysiological clues; but the educational philosopher tends to focus on the practical judgments that have to be made in the actual conduct of practice. Paul Hirst has written that such judgments are formed "in the midst of a complex network of understanding which cannot be adequately and formally expressed" (Hirst 1967, p. 83). It may be, to use the novelist Doris Grumbach's metaphor, the teacher's "compost heap." A diversity of beliefs make up what Hirst described as a network: beliefs having to do with the nature of human reality, knowing, valuing, the social context, teaching itself. Relevant concepts and knowledge-claims derived from psychology and the social sciences are part of the complex; so may be analytic and critical modes of dealing with language and argument. There may be some incidental concern with such matters as mind-body relations or what Hilary Putnam calls "functional isomorphism" (Putnam 1984, p. 292); but if there is, it is likely to connect with other strands of the network in the same way as does the idea of what it means to be human and the degree to which the learner may be ascribed a sense of moral agency. A composite theory may derive from the network: a theory concerned with specifically educational questions having to do with the intentional activities conducted in classrooms, many of them having to do with the growth of mind.

Perhaps because of the contemporary preoccupation with the cognitive and the technical, educators are turning their attention from "adjustment" and simple "preparation" to mindfulness, or what R. S. Peters calls "qualities of mind" (Peters 1975, p. 22); but again, their concern is for what can be done to develop and enhance these qualities, not to explain what they are. Their practical judgments refer to distinctive modes of action and transaction taking place in specific contexts, often extending beyond the walls of the classroom and the school. They have to do largely with what is audible and visible, with what finds articulation in speech-acts and bodily gestures. This does not, it must be stressed, entail a mainly behaviorist view, since, more often than not, those being observed are thought to be conscious of what they are doing, capable of moral agency. There are those, too, who conceive of the mind as Dewey does, as "primarily a verb," and who therefore direct their attention to the ways in which people "deal consciously and expressly with the situations" in which they find themselves (Dewey 1934, p. 263). Again, instead of a concern for explanation, we find an orientation to the ways in which individuals act, speak, follow rules, interpret what is said to them, engage in inquiries, apply concepts, use tactics, make connections, pose questions, try things out, communicate with others, make decisions, and account for themselves.

The signal problems with regard to the growth of mind center on the

question of voluntariness and the obstacles to the release of preferences. The technicism of the present, the conservatism of the grass
roots, and current definitions of "excellence" as measured achievement all stand in the way of a recognition of students' sense of agency.
Educational philosophers continue to link their concern for mind and
mindfulness with the discovery of ways of engaging learners as persons capable of independent judgment. Israel Scheffler, for example,
has said that teachers are required to acknowledge the young's demands for good reasons and their capacity to evaluate the reasons
offered them for what happens in the schools. He stresses the teacher's
need to make accessible his or her reasons and purposes for getting
students to do things, as well as the hope that some of the teacher's
reasons will become the students' reasons (Scheffler 1960, p. 58). This
suggests again that teaching for mindfulness entails far more than the
mere transmission of skills and information. If the cultivation of mind
is taken seriously, efforts must be made to help students understand the
rationale for their acquiring certain skills, knowledge, and modes of
conduct. It is a matter of their being able to reflect upon their own
learning, to think about their own thinking even in the face of "high
tech" and consumerist socioeconomic demands.

Related to all of this is the problem of moving or provoking the
young to break through horizons at various moments of their lives.
There is a time for moving into the life of language, for learning to use
the range of symbol systems. There is a time for being initiated into the
forms of knowledge and into the several knowledge fields. There is a
time, as Alfred North Whitehead writes, for achieving the kind of
"freedom in the presence of knowledge" that can only come through
"discipline in the acquirement of ordered fact" (Whitehead 1949,
p. 41). Whitehead saw wisdom "as the way in which knowledge is
held . . . its selection for the determination of relevant issues, its employment to add value to our immediate experience." Carrying further
the notion of learning as cognitive action, he writes: "An education
which does not begin by evoking initiative and end by encouraging it
must be wrong. For its whole aim is the production of active wisdom"
(Whitehead 1949, p. 48).

When we look among educational thinkers today (at least outside
the stark realms of behaviorism), we find an abandonment of old notions of simple receptivity or of the mind as *tabula rasa*. Outmoded
notions of the mind as "ghost in the machine" (Ryle 1949, p. 15), or
empty container, or flower in need of watering have generally been set
aside. Computer and machine analogies are used more frequently, it is

true; paradigms are sometimes found in artificial intelligence and the heuristic reasoning associated with some of its forms. Jerry Fodor's conceptions of inner codes and the "language of thought" (Fodor 1975, pp. 198ff.) have awakened some interest, as has the view that "cognitive processes" can be thought of in terms of information flow, hypothesis testing, inference, and decision making. This kind of thinking, however, is thinking according to analogy; and it remains difficult to see how it can give rise to theories of practice, much less theories of mind. Fodor has also written about neural systems of representation, structures resembling natural languages but designed for computation rather than communication; but this does not seem to have affected educational thinking. Problems of knowledge representation are, nevertheless, raised with increasing frequency, especially when teachers are asked to concern themselves with representing their subject matters in ways that might mesh with diverse students' conceptions of the world. The connection between linguistic and pictorial representations may soon begin to awaken curiosity, along with the idea that interpreting the unfamiliar involves bringing to bear "the background of related representations we already understand, along with any additional knowledge and skill we can press into service" (Elgin 1984, p. 925). It would appear that present efforts to understand what is involved in making "correct" interpretations have educational relevance, but thus far this aspect of the development of mind has not appeared to influence thinking about what should be done in classrooms.

There does, however, seem to be a growing interest in interpretive knowing and the pursuit of meanings, with an accompanying interest in vantage point, intersubjectivity, and location in the social world (Taylor 1977, pp. 101–131). If reality can be understood to be interpreted experience, then participation in the perspectives and points of view made available through the culture must have a good deal to do with the growth of mind. In education, there is a presumption that the culture has the means of empowering people to become mindful; and most educators act, on some level, in the light of George Herbert Mead's view that "mind arises in the social process only when that process as a whole enters into, or is present in, the experience of any one of the given individuals involved in that process. When this occurs the individual becomes self-conscious and has a mind . . ." (Mead 1948, p. 134). The recognition that mind is a function of communication and social relations has made possible a more or less general acceptance of the "sociocentric" approach to knowledge (Soltis 1981, p. 97). Stemming in part from Alfred Schutz's conception of social reality and the social world (Schutz 1964) and from Peter Berger and Thomas Luckmann's studies of "the social construction of reality" (Berger and Luckmann 1966), this approach connects knowledge to the knower, views knowledge as embedded in social life, and grounds it in common-sense or everyday reality. The mind, then, must be seen to develop by means of self-reflective engagement in the intersubjective world.

Interpretive engagement with a range of cultural perspectives, with the various disciplines, leads to the funding of more and more meanings. It may be said that *these funded meanings constitute what educators think of as mind.* The more there are, the richer and more variegated is the background for new encounters with things, events, and ideas. The more meanings have been accumulated, the more representations there are, and this suggests that more dimensions of lived experience have been interpreted or named. The individual learner is then in a position to select those aspects of reality still to be inquired into, thematized, evaluated, *understood.* He or she has internalized certain conceptual networks, learned various "cognitive styles" (Schutz 1967, pp. 230ff.), and come to realize some of the multiple ways of directing attention to the world.

What characterizes this account and others that stress interpretation (or the hermeneutic approach) is the concern for the knower's vantage point, location, and grounding in an intersubjective, common-sense world. Currently more widespread educational views focus with greater exclusivity on the development of mind as it relates to the conceptual structuring of experience. Paul Hirst, treating liberal education as education in the forms of knowledge, says explicitly that mind develops through mastery of "the complex ways of understanding experience which man has achieved, which are publicly specifiable and gained through learning. An education in these terms does indeed develop its related abilities and qualities of mind, for the mind will be characterized to a greater or lesser degree by the features of the understanding it seeks" (Hirst 1975, p. 9). Each form of knowledge involves the development of judgment, creative imagination, and so on; but it is primarily the cognitive framework (governed by public criteria) that ought to pattern and order human life. Hirst marks the connection between mastery of the symbol systems or forms of knowledge and participation in the culture's "conversation"; but he pays little heed to lived perspectives, work, intentions, everyday and commonsense reality. Critics point to the minimal concern for emotions, for attitudes, for ordinary life, for social concern (Martin 1981, pp. 57–58). They say

Hirst pays too little attention to the aliveness and sense of disclosure that interpretive engagements allow.

What Merleau-Ponty calls the "landscape"—the perceiving and imagining that compose the ground for knowing and the known—goes unheeded, as do the passion and interrogations that the embodied consciousness brings into the world (Merleau-Ponty 1964, pp. 20–23). In "Eye and Mind," Merleau-Ponty challenges the "artificialism" of certain scientific claims, along with the tendency to conceptualize human reality on the basis "of a few abstract indices." He writes:

Scientific thinking, a thinking which looks on from above, and thinks of the object-in-general, must return to the "there is" which underlies it; to the site, the soil of the sensible and opened world such as it is in our life and for our body—not that possible body which we may legitimately think of as an information machine but that actual body I call mine, this sentinel standing quietly at the command of my words and my acts. Further, associated bodies must be brought forward along with my body . . . the others who haunt me and whom I haunt. . . . (1964, pp. 160–161)

And it is the *there is*, for him, that must be taken into account if we are to grasp the workings of soul or mind. Concerned as Merleau-Ponty was with perception and the perspectival, with vision and the visible world, he could never identify the growth of mind solely with "the features of understanding." Nor could he ever conceive fixity or completeness. Mind and body were integrally related; both were entangled in being, in the world; both were enmeshed in intersubjectivity.

With this view and the views that focus on the pursuit of meaning as background, I want to turn to some works of literature that have to do with the growth of mind. The styles, the periods, even the genres of the works I will use differ from one another. What Wordsworth, Joyce, and Alice Walker have in common, though, is a capacity to transmute aspects of lived reality in such a way as to make them present to a reader's consciousness, to offer them for the reader's grasping and achieving. Each one, of course, is creating an "as if," an imaginary world, one that can only be entered by readers willing to set aside the taken-for-granted and the demonstrably known and to re-view in some manner what they believe, perceive, feel, as well as know. The disclosures made possible are not to be seen as superior to, or competitive with, validated knowledge about the human psyche, mind, or consciousness. They show forth; they make visible and palpable what is, in other domains, explained and described. They allow for a type of understanding that may provide a ground and launching place for personal inquiries into the life of the mind. Other literary artists might be used; these are only exemplary. The point of turning to them is that they have the power of helping us recover some lost spontaneity, some authentic sense of what it is like to grow into the world as mindful creatures. I believe that, perhaps particularly within educational contexts, we have finally to choose our stance on the basis of our own memories, our own lived lives. Imaginative literature has the peculiar capacity to impart an intelligibility to them, to release new possibilities of thought, to open doors.

It happens that each of the works mentioned below presents young persons thinking in terms of increasingly complex metaphors that allow them to find new patterns of "congruence" (Ricoeur 1981, p. 145), of significance in their own experience as they grow. Each work presents children and then young people using their productive imaginations, summoning up absent images, synthesizing, reaching out toward possibility. Each one confirms the notion that metaphormaking and imagining are integral to the growth of mind. Each one suggests, as discursive works cannot, a crucial interrelationship among feeling, metaphor, and imagination that ought not to be overlooked when the knower is being provoked (by a teacher, for instance) to engage the known.

Wordsworth's *The Prelude* is subtitled *Growth of a Poet's Mind* (Wordsworth 1954, pp. 203–438); but it remains, nevertheless, paradigmatic for all human growth. It is a poem of remembering and recovery, since, in order to overcome a midlife discontent and frustration, the poet returns to his childhood home. He physically goes back to the Lake Country, and the encounter with that original landscape releases memories for him, feelings that cluster about the images he discovers, imaginative orderings and reorderings for the sake of understanding, making sense. Not only does he see the fields and mountains again; not only does he walk among them. He is able to summon up the "knots of grass" and the "slippery rock" he clung to when he went to plunder a bird's nest (p. 213), the "black and huge" peak he saw when he stole a boat one night and went rowing on the silent lake (p. 215). Each time, he recalls, there was a sense of expansion: the sound of a "loud, dry wind," the "dim and undetermined sense of unknown modes of being."

At the end of Book 1, having recollected "hours that have the charm of visionary things," his mind feels revived, and he is prepared to tell the story of his life (p. 222). And so he does, first about education and solitude, then about gradually enlarging experiences in engagement with others. He tells of encounters with literature, mathematics, the French Revolution, the city crowds. He speaks of the confusion of the city, the crowds "amid the same perpetual whirl of trivial objects," of the oppression that weighs down on everyone, of how "unmanageable" a sight it was, and meaningless. Then he is able to summon up the imaginative power which "sees parts as parts, but with a feeling for the whole" (p. 332); and he links attention, "comprehensiveness and memory," all stemming from experiences of childhood with a sharply sensed natural world. If a capacity to enter into "correspondence with the talking world" (p. 418), to ponder all the ways in which one has come to construe reality signifies the development (and yes, the creation) of a mind, then the Wordsworthian rendering does indeed highlight the ways in which imaging and imagining play a part, along with metaphor making, feeling, and memory. Book 13, "Imagination," concludes:

> Moreover, each man's Mind is to herself
> Witness and judge; and I remember well
> That in life's every-day appearances
> I seemed about this time to gain clear sight
> Of a new world—a world, too, that was fit
> To be transmitted, and to other eyes
> Made visible; as ruled by those fixed laws
> Whence spiritual dignity originates,
> Which do both give it being and maintain
> A balance, an ennobling interchange
> Of action from without and from within;
> The excellence, pure function, and best power
> Both of the object seen, and eye that sees. (p. 424)

Wordsworth is speaking of self-reflection and self-knowledge, of perspectives on what might be, what "was fit to be transmitted" and communicated. He is speaking of the transaction between the outer and inner, of "action," of the continuing dialectical interchange out of which each one's mind might grow. He is speaking of maturity; he ends, finally, with a paean to the mind.

From quite another standpoint, we see similar themes in James Joyce's *A Portrait of the Artist as a Young Man* (1947). From our first introduction to the consciousness of the infant Stephen Daedalus, we become aware of the degree to which the stream of events is grasped by means of metaphor. Even the free associations emerge from the work of imagination: "There was a picture of the earth green and the clouds maroon. That was like the two brushes in Dante's press, the brush with the green velvet back for Parnell and the brush with the maroon velvet back for Michael Davitt" (p. 15). It may be recalled how Stephen traces his membership from the "class of elements" at Clongowes Wood College to the universe, how wondering about the universe makes him think of what lay around it, something he admits only God could do. And then he ponders God's name, and languages, and naming generally; and he grows gradually toward naming, and words, and a world rendered "through the prism of a language manycoloured and richly storied" (p. 166) and, eventually, into an exorcism through the use of language, through seeing, through a desire to encounter "the reality of experience" (p. 253). The growth of mind is deeply entwined with sensing, perceiving, remembering, imagining, listening, and saying; and it culminates in anticipation, expectation, in a desire (at some future time) to recreate the conscience of the race. Again, it is impossible to grasp mind as developing apart from lived life and the stream of consciousness; it is difficult to grasp mind as developing without imagining consequences rather than antecedents.

Unlike Stephen Daedalus, the child in Alice Walker's *The Color Purple* (1983) has little language, at least at the start. Victimized, made into an object, she writes letters to God without daring to speak in the first person. She begins to create herself as a person as she is moved to wonder, to seek out images, to name. The first time she is taken to buy a dress for herself, she thinks "what color Shug Avery would wear. She like a queen to me so I say to Kate, Somethin purple, maybe little red in it too. But us look an look an no purple" (p. 28). When she does meet the blues singer, Shug, she is urged to affirm herself, to be, and finally to stop seeing God as an old censorious white man. Shug tells her: "My first step from the old white man was trees. Then air. Then birds. Then other people." And Celie says: "Well, let us talk and talk bout God, but I'm still adrift. Trying to chase that old white man out of my head. I been so busy thinking bout him I never truly notice nothing God make. Not a blade of corn (how it do that?). Not the color purple (where it come from?). Not the little wildflowers. Nothing. Now that my eyes are opening, I feels like a fool" (p. 179). The necessary questions, the perplexities, arise out of the overcoming of victimization, out of restlessness, out of imaging. Mind is presented as emergent here, as a human being is released to see, to name, to make sense.

Bruner, discussing the growth of intellect and the capacity to construct models of the world, writes about the three systems human beings possess for representing reality.

One is through action. We know some things by knowing how to do them. . . . A second way of knowing is through imagery and those products of mind that, in effect, stop the action and summarize it in a representing ikon. . . . Finally, there is representation by symbol, of which the typecase is language with its rules for forming sentences not only about what exists in experience but, by its powerful combinatorial techniques, for forming equally good ones about what might or might not exist. (Bruner 1973, pp. 7–8)

He, too, seems to see the integral relation between the growing of mind and imagining, moving towards "what might or might not exist." Indeed, Mary Warnock calls imagination a "power in the mind," with its impetus coming from "the emotions as much as from the reason, from the heart as much as the head" (Warnock 1978, p. 196). She also turns to Wordsworth in making the significant point that most people have a sense that "there is always more to experience, and more in what we experience than we can predict" (p. 202). Without this sense, she believes, experience becomes pointless and boring; and this suggests a reason for educators to include a concern for imagination in their concern for the development of mind. It is imagination, she says, that allows meanings to spring up around us, that permits us to see meanings *in* objects and events. If it is indeed the case that accumulating meanings are what constitute mind, then the nurturing of imagination cannot be separated from the nurturing of mindfulness.

For Dewey, imagination is the gateway through which meanings derived from prior experience find their way into present transactions. He says that "the conscious adjustment of the new and the old *is* imagination." And then he writes about the gap that always exists between what we experience in the here and now and the funded meanings that make it possible for us to grasp and interpret what is happening. "Because of this gap," he says, "all conscious perception involves a risk; it is a venture into the unknown, for as it assimilates the present to the past it also brings about some reconstruction of that past" (Dewey 1934, p. 272). We can see this in the imaginative works already referred to; it is played out in novel after novel—*Moby-Dick, War and Peace, The Great Gatsby, The Magic Mountain, The Plague, The Name of the Rose*. Mind, with its imaginative power, continues to open new perspectives, new ways of understanding what has been, even as it reaches forward into the unknown, towards what might and ought to be.

In a different idiom, Merleau-Ponty makes kindred points, while placing an even greater stress upon the perceived landscape and children's distinctive ways of configuring through imagination. "What is called *imagination*," he writes, "is an emotional conduct. Consequently here again we found ourselves, as it were, *beneath* the relation of the knowing subject to the known object. We had to do with a primordial operation by which the child organizes the imaginary, just as he organizes the perceived" (1964, p. 98). As Merleau-Ponty sees it, the perceived or appearing world is presupposed by knowing and communication. Moreover, the perceptual life is preserved even while it is transformed; "and the characteristic operation of the mind is in the movement by which we recapture our corporeal existence and use it to symbolize instead of merely to co-exist" (1964, p. 7). Mind and rationality, for him, are built upon perceptual foundations and the configurations created by perception and imagination.

It is by being unrestrictedly and unreservedly what I am at present that I have a chance of moving forward; it is by living my time that I am able to understand other times, by plunging into the present and the world, by taking on deliberately what I am fortuitously, by willing what I will and doing what I do, that I can go further. . . . We are *true* through and through, and have with us, by the mere fact of belonging to the world and not merely being in the world in the way that things are, all that we need to transcend ourselves. (1967, p. 456)

Again, it is in belonging to the world and seeking to transcend it that mind can grow and do its work.

In education, the confrontation must come first, the questioning against the sedimentation and configurations of the individual's lived life. Metaphors past and present feed into the question. As in the case of Wordsworth's poet, imagination may open the way for the interrogation that leads to a quest for intelligibility. That is why it is so important for teachers to devise situations that release memory, feelings, and vision—situations in which students can become conscious of their own consciousness, of the sense in which they belong to the world and to one another. Encounters with the arts have to play a part: situations of making, situations of attending. Play and speech have to play a part, allowing people to find out what they think by articulating it in words, games, and gestures. Made aware of their original landscapes—the sounds of winds, the shapes of peaks—in background consciousness, they reach out toward possibility. Reaching out, of course, they are conscious of absence, of what they are not yet, of what they do not yet know. And it is the sense of absence that propels the questions. They do not occur to those at ease in the common-sensible, submerged in everydayness, in what phenomenologists call the "natural attitude." It goes without saying that the person must have developed sufficiently to be living in language as an open system, must have arrived at the point where he or she can thematize or symbolize that which the consciousness is grasping. Seeing perspectivally, from his or her own standpoint, the person must feel the need for other standpoints. That may be when the person feels interrogated. Seeking meanings, he or she may extend into other languages that multiply perspectives, that open up the multiplex world.

Yes, there are differences among philosophers where education and the development of mind are concerned. Analytical philosophers like Gilbert Ryle, R. S. Peters, and Hilary Putnam lay primary stress on language even as they speak of consciousness. Peters, for example, has spoken of "consciousness at the hall-mark of mind" (Peters 1978, p. 47); consciousness, as he views it, is the soil in which "public modes of thought and awareness . . . mainly enshrined in language" take root. It is these public modes of thought and awareness that "provide avenues of access to a public world" (Peters 1967, p. 20). Not surprisingly, the consummation of education is participation in the "conversation" mentioned above, the conversation in which people who possess the requisite knowledge, understanding, and sensitivity can take part. Peters is joined in this view by Paul Hirst and Richard Rorty (Rorty 1979), both of whom turn to the work of Michael Oakeshott, who writes: "Education, properly speaking, is an initiation into the skill and partnership of this conversation in which we learn to recognize the voices, to distinguish the proper occasions of utterance, and in which we acquire the intellectual and moral habits appropriate to conversation. And it is this conversation which, in the end, gives place and character to every human activity and utterance" (Oakeshott 1962, pp. 198–199).

Here is where the language philosophers and the phenomenologists tend to part, where both education and the growth of mind are concerned. As we have already noted, consciousness is not viewed by the phenomenologist (or by Dewey) as primarily a knowing consciousness. It is, rather, a living consciousness, a perceiving consciousness, and (for Merleau-Ponty) an embodied consciousness. For such thinkers, consciousness must be understood as the way in which human beings thrust into and find their way through the world, and such precognitive acts as those associated with imagining and perceiving precede and ground the cognitive. This is in no sense an irrationalism, a noncognitive, or a "mindless" approach to being. Not only does it overcome the subject/object separation when it comes to comprehending the knowing and the known; it allows, I think, for the inclusion of modalities of awareness, those associated with becoming, with both the development and creation of mind. "To say that there exists rationality," writes Merleau-Ponty, "is to say that perspectives blend, perceptions confirm each other, a meaning emerges" (Merleau-Ponty 1967, p. xix). And this seems to me to be of the first importance where teaching is concerned.

And finally, there is the matter of the common world. As we have seen, there is some agreement that mind is a mode of conduct that can appear only within live contexts of communication and relationship. Within educational frameworks, this ought to imply an always-increasing attentiveness to dialogue, to a continually enriched inter-subjective world. It ought also to highlight the diversities of mindfulness likely to appear in any classroom and the importance of releasing the young to thematize, to articulate what they remember and what they live. It is from their own lived worlds, I would insist, that they can be ushered into the various provinces of meaning to diversify their perspectives, to understand more, to interpret more variously. These provinces of meaning, for Alfred Schutz, "are merely names for different tensions of one and the same consciousness" (Schutz 1967, p. 258). They all belong to the same stream; they can be remembered and reproduced. The crucial point (and this may be the true consummation of the growth of mind) is that *the meanings disclosed can be communicated in ordinary language within ordinary life*. For some, the language may be gesture; for others, it may be song; for still others, it may be quantification; for most, it will be verbal translation, extending the interpretations of the real. More than conversation, more than commentary, the transactions may lead to what Schutz has metaphorically called "making music together" (Schutz 1964, pp. 159–178). There will be communication and a continually widening sphere of meaning, as minds inform intersubjective action and living worlds are transcended and transformed.

References

Berger, P. and Luckmann, T. 1966. *The Social Construction of Reality*. Garden City, N.Y.: Anchor Books.

Bruner, J. 1973. *The Relevance of Education*. New York: Norton Library.

Dewey, J. 1916. *Democracy and Education*. New York: Macmillan Co.

———. 1934. *Art as Experience*. New York: Minton Balch & Co.

———. 1960. "Philosophies of Freedom." *John Dewey on Experience, Nature, and Freedom*, pp. 46–53. Edited by R. Bernstein. New York: Liberal Arts Press.

Elgin, C. 1984. "Representation, Comprehension, and Competence." *Social Research* 51:4.

Fodor, J. 1975. *The Language of Thought*. New York: Crowell.

Gruber, H. and Voneche, J., eds. 1977. *The Essential Piaget*. New York: Basic Books.

Hirst, P. 1966. "Philosophy and Educational Theory." *Philosophy and Education*, pp. 3–17. Edited by I. Scheffler. Boston: Allyn and Bacon.

———. 1975. "Liberal Education and the Nature of Knowledge." *Education and Reason*, pp. 83–96. Edited by R. F. Dearden, P. H. Hirst, and R. S. Peters. London: Routledge & Kegan Paul.

Joyce, J. 1947. *A Portrait of the Artist as a Young Man*. New York: Charles Scribner and Son.

Martin, J. 1981. "Needed: A Paradigm for Liberal Education." *Philosophy and Education*, pp. 37–59. Edited by J. F. Soltis. Chicago: University of Chicago Press.

Mead, G. 1948. *Mind, Self and Society*. Chicago: University of Chicago Press.

Merleau-Ponty, M. 1964. *The Primacy of Perception*. Evanston, Ill.: Northwestern University Press.

———. 1967. *Phenomenology of Perception*. New York: Humanities Press.

———. 1968. *The Structure of Behavior*. Boston: Beacon Press.

Miller, J. 1983. *States of Mind*. New York: Pantheon Books.

Oakeshott, M. 1962. *Rationalism in Politics*. London: Methuen.

Peters, R. 1967. "What Is an Educational Process?" *The Concept of Education*, pp. 1–23. Edited by R. S. Peters. New York: Humanities Press.

———. 1975. "Education and Human Development." *Education and Reason*. Edited by R. F. Dearden, P. H. Hirst, and R. S. Peters. London: Routledge & Kegan Paul.

———. 1978. *Ethics and Education*. London: George Allen & Unwin.

Putnam, H. 1984. *Mind, Language and Reality*. New York: Cambridge University Press.

Ricoeur, P. 1981. "The Metaphorical Process as Cognition, Imagination, and Feeling." *Metaphor*, pp. 103–118. Edited by S. Sacks. Chicago: University of Chicago Press.

Rorty, R. 1980. *Philosophy and the Mirror of Nature*. Princeton, N.J.: Princeton University Press.

Ryle, G. 1949. *The Concept of Mind*. New York: Barnes and Noble.

———. 1967. "Teaching and Training." *The Concept of Education*, pp. 105–119. Edited by R. S. Peters. New York: Humanities Press.

Scheffler, I. 1960. *The Language of Teaching*. Springfield, Ill.: Charles Thomas.

Schutz, A. 1962. Collected Papers I, *The Problem of Social Reality*. The Hague: Martinus Nijhoff.

———. 1964. Collected Papers II, *Studies in Social Theory*. The Hague: Martinus Nijhoff.

Soltis, J. 1981. "Education and the Concept of Knowledge." *Philosophy and Education*, pp. 95–113. Edited by J. F. Soltis. Chicago: University of Chicago Press.

Taylor, C. 1977. "Interpretation and the Sciences of Man." *Understanding and Social Inquiry*, pp. 71–89. Edited by F. R. Dallmayr and T. A. McCarthy. South Bend, Ind.: University of Notre Dame Press.

Vygotsky, L. 1978. *Mind in Society*. Cambridge, Mass.: Harvard University Press.

Walker, A. 1983. *The Color Purple*. New York: Washington Square Press.

Warnock, M. 1978. *Imagination*. Berkeley: University of California Press.

Whitehead, A. 1949. *The Aims of Education*. New York: Mentor Books.

Wordsworth, W. 1954. *The Prelude*. Edited by Carlos Baker. New York: Holt, Rinehart and Winston.

Notes on Contributors

Richard M. Caplan, M.D., Professor of Dermatology, Associate Dean for Continuing Medical Education, and founding director of the Program in Medical Humanities at the University of Iowa College of Medicine, organized the symposium which gave rise to this collection. He has published extensively in the literature of dermatology, continuing medical education, and the medical humanities.

Hilary Putnam, Ph.D., Professor of Philosophy, Harvard University, is a leading American philosopher with a special interest in the history of ideas and the history of science. He is the author of many books, among them *Mathematics, Matter and Method*; *Meaning and the Moral Sciences*; *Mind, Language, and Reality*; *Realism and Reason*; *Philosophy of Logic*; *Philosophy of Mathematics*; and *Reason, Truth and History*.

Julian Jaynes, Ph.D., Professor of Psychology, Princeton University, is best known for his controversial book *The Origin of Consciousness in the Breakdown of the Bicameral Mind*. Although his academic position is in the Department of Psychology, his erudition and expertise clearly stem from, and branch into, philosophy, linguistics, archeology, literature, and history.

Antonio R. Damasio, M.D., Ph.D., Professor of Neurology and Chief of the Division of Behavioral Neurology at the University of Iowa, is internationally known for his numerous investigations in neurobiology and clinical medicine, especially Alzheimer's disease. His presentation focuses on the "scientific" end of the spectrum represented at this highly interdisciplinary symposium.

David B. Morris, Ph.D., a former faculty member of the University of Iowa's Department of English, now lives in Kalamazoo, Michigan. In addition to many scholarly articles, he has received plaudits for his 1983 book *Alexander Pope*, published by the Harvard University Press.

In recent years he has developed a special interest in the language used by writers and patients to express pain.

D. N. Perkins, Ph.D., is a senior research associate working in the Graduate School of Education at Harvard University. His many publications include *The Arts and Cognition, Teaching Thinking,* and *The Mind's Best Work,* growing from his extensive work regarding the development and expression of imagination and creativity, particularly among gifted children. Dr. Perkins did his doctoral work in computer science and artificial intelligence.

Doris Grumbach, Ph.D., is a successful novelist and literary critic. She appears regularly as a commentator on public radio and has served as visiting professor and director of the University of Iowa Writers' Workshop. Her published novels include *The Spoil of the Flowers; The Short Throat, the Tender Mouth; The Company She Kept; Chamber Music; The Missing Person;* and in 1984, *The Ladies.*

Maxine Greene, Ph.D., a philosopher of education at Columbia University, has an unusual breadth of background in literature and the humanities. Her published books include *Existential Encounters for Teachers, Landscapes of Learning, The Public School and the Private Vision,* and *Teacher as Stranger.*